CAN
CONFLICT
END?

ALSO BY THE AUTHOR

Freedom from the Known

The First and Last Freedom

The Flight of the Eagle

What Are You Doing with Your Life?

What Are You Looking For?

CAN CONFLICT END?

J. KRISHNAMURTI

Edited by David Skitt and Duncan Toms

RIDER

Rider, an imprint of Ebury Publishing
20 Vauxhall Bridge Road
London SW1V 2SA

Rider is part of the Penguin Random House group of companies
whose addresses can be found at global.penguinrandomhouse.com

First published by Rider in 2023

www.penguin.co.uk

A CIP catalogue record for this book is available from the British Library

ISBN 9781846047558

Typeset in 11.5/15 pt Bembo Book MT Pro by Jouve (UK), Milton Keynes
Printed and bound in Great Britain by Clays Ltd, Elcograf S.p.A.

The authorised representative in the EEA is Penguin Random House Ireland,
Morrison Chambers, 32 Nassau Street, Dublin D02 YH68

Penguin Random House is committed to a sustainable future
for our business, our readers and our planet. This book is made
from Forest Stewardship Council® certified paper.

Contents

Introduction by David Skitt   1

PART ONE
Public Talks

1. Deal with facts. Opinions cause conflict.   7

2. What is the deep function of the brain?
   Obviously not to live in conflict.   23

3. The self, in its isolating state, seeks
   security in illusions.   38

4. Conflict causes deterioration of the brain.   55

5. The common ground on which all human
   beings stand.   68

6. Religion and meditation. Seeing when thought
   is a source of conflict. The ending of
   psychological measurement.   81

PART TWO
Questions and Answers

Introduction by J. Krishnamurti   101

7. You have said to us 'You are the world and you are totally responsible for the whole of mankind.' How can this idea be justified on a rational, objective, sane basis?   103

8. What is psychological time, and why is it a source of conflict?   107

9. If two people have a relationship of conflict and pain, can they resolve it or must the relationship end? And to have a good relationship, isn't it necessary for both to change?   112

10. Would you please go into what you mean by reading the book of your life at a glance or with a single look?   118

11. You said it is necessary to have no opinions about anything, but I feel it is necessary. Mustn't one say something about what is taking place, or perhaps do something?   121

12. After listening to you and thinking about these matters on my own, how am I to really not just solve my problems but radically bring about a change in my life?   125

13. How do you know what you are saying is true?   129

Sources   135

INTRODUCTION

Throughout his life, Krishnamurti maintained that the extent of human conflict showed that something was 'radically amiss'. But his account of its causes went well beyond a simple moral judgement. To him, it was obvious that rival religious beliefs and political ideologies, often inflamed with nationalism, were clearly divisive and embittered by territorial claims and ruthless economic competition. As we have seen in our own times, even after a worldwide natural disaster like a pandemic, the obvious need for working together in a shared plight easily succumbs to nationalist ambition. And now the war in Ukraine.

Krishnamurti also saw a far deeper and long-lasting source of conflict in our failure to see that action driven by thought based on past experience, and on selective memory and projection of that experience, is always bound to cause strife in human relationships, whether between two people or the groups of us we call nations. Experience, which is inevitably limited, can never respond fully to the new and unforeseen that life constantly presents us with. Yet we still keep trying to make it do so. A further major factor of conflict, he contends, lies in thought making images of others and oneself, which are bound, again, by the limited nature of the experience they are based on, to be contentious stereotypes.

The vital and natural question Krishnamurti then asks and wants us all to ask is: If thought and experience fall short in human relationships, what are we left with? The implications of this question are discussed in detail and repeatedly in this series of six talks.

More than 70 books of Krishnamurti's talks, dialogues and writings have been published and translated worldwide. So what will a 'seasoned' reader find that is new in this one? Certainly, familiar themes are worded anew and amplified. But there is also fresh and intricate discussion of the psychological impact of the sound of words, the 'space' needed in listening to words and the 'closeness' with which one approaches a problem. What is there to discover here for someone new to Krishnamurti? As well as the points already mentioned, these talks cover many of his major themes: the focus on facts, *what is* instead of *what should be*; time and thought; the inherent limitation of human knowledge; physical and psychological security; the isolating effects of the self; suffering; fear; intelligence, love and compassion.

Can Conflict End? consists of two parts: the public talks in Part One and the questions and answers in Part Two. These provide a revealing contrast between the necessary formality of a public talk and the easy-going informality, which Krishnamurti clearly enjoyed, of responding to very challenging questions.

David Skitt

PART ONE

Public Talks

Chapter 1

Deal with facts. Opinions cause conflict.

We are going to talk over together many serious things. These gatherings are not intellectual or emotional entertainment, they are serious, and we are exploring, investigating and inquiring together. I am not putting forth ideas, but rather we are going to observe facts. The word *fact* means that which has been done in the past or that which is happening now. The future is non-fact; it is a hope, an idea, a concept, but what is actually a fact is that which is happening and that which has happened. So, we are going to deal only with facts, not with concepts, ideas, speculations, however philosophical or interesting they may be. We are going to consider together the fact of what we are, the fact of what is happening around us in the world, and the fact that most of us are concerned only with ourselves.

We live in a world that has no peace. There is such chaos, disorder, great danger, terrorism and threats of war – these are all facts. Is it possible to live our daily lives peacefully in this world, with its turmoil and toil and all the problems we have? The politicians, the Christian hierarchy, the Hindus, Buddhists and Muslims talk of peace, but actually there is none. And peace is necessary for us in order to grow, to flower, to understand, to have time to look around, to explore ourselves and what we can find there. We need to have peace, but not in the sense of freedom *from* something. The interval between two wars, between two quarrels, two problems, or a sense of physical relaxation, is not peace. Peace is something much more fundamental, much deeper than the superficial peace you have, or think you have.

We are going to talk over as two friends whether it is possible to live in peace both inwardly, that is psychologically, and outwardly. We may want peace, see the need for it, but we do not live peaceful lives. And the world is preparing for war, with ideologies fighting each other; politicians and governments do not consider humanity but the extension of power. We cannot look for peace to come from politicians and governments. Neither can it come from the religions, despite their talk about it.

Where do you find peace? Because you must see very clearly that without it, we are like animals, destroying each other – and we are also destroying the earth, the ocean, the air. Politically and religiously, we have looked to leaders to unify and bring about peace, but they have not succeeded either. Governments, politicians, religious leaders, peace movements – none of them have brought peace to human beings, to you and me. So, where do we find it? Without the fundamental necessity of peace, we cannot possibly understand the greater things of life. So together we will go into this, not verbally, not intellectually, but to find out for ourselves – without any guide, any leadership, any priest, any psychologist, because all that has failed – whether we can have peace in the world and in ourselves.

First of all, can we have peace in ourselves? *Peace* is a rather complicated word. We give it different meanings depending on our mood, our intellectual concepts, or various romantic and emotional interpretations. Let us not give it various meanings but grasp the significance and depth of the word. Peace of mind, like physical peace, is not merely freedom from something, but the ending of all conflict. That is real peace, not only in ourselves but with our neighbours and with the world, peace with the environment, the ecology, peace that is deep-rooted, unshakeable, not a superficial, passing thing but peace of timeless depth.

Peace has been sought through meditation, and all over the world that has been one of its purposes. But meditation is not the search for peace, it is something very different, which we will go into presently.

So, what is peace and how can we lay and establish its foundation so that we build on it, psychologically speaking? Remember, we are talking this over together; I am not scoring points. I am not an authority but in talking over together, things become very clear. If we can talk over together without any bias, any prejudice, having no conclusions or concepts about peace, we can go into it together. But if you have opinions about peace, what peace should be, then your inquiry stops.

Opinions have no value, though the whole world is run on them. Opinions are limited. Your opinion, or my opinion, the opinions of totalitarian and so-called democratic governments, or the opinions of the clergy, are all limited. So are your judgements and opinions about values. I hope we understand the meaning of the word *limited*. When you think about yourself from morning to night, as most people do, it is very, very limited. When you say you are American or British, it is very limited. So, opinions are limited. When you see that clearly, you do not cling to them or the values those opinions have created. Your opinion versus another opinion does not bring about peace.

That is what is happening in the world: one ideology versus another – communist, socialist, democratic and so on. So please understand, if I may say it again, that we are talking over together, and if you are sticking to your opinion and I am sticking to mine, we shall never meet. There must be freedom from opinion and its values.

Can we go on from there? So that you are not holding onto your opinions and using them as rods to beat or kill each other, but seeing that the opinions you have are limited and therefore must inevitably bring about conflict. If you hold onto your limited conclusions and experience, and another holds onto theirs, there is not only conflict but wars and destruction. If you see that very clearly, then opinions become very, very superficial; they have no meaning. So, please, when you are inquiring about what is peace, and whether you can live in peace, don't have opinions about it. Be free to inquire, and in that inquiry act. The very inquiry *is* action. It is not that you inquire first and then act, but in the process of inquiry you are acting. I hope again that it is clear, that there must be freedom to inquire. It is the very basis of peace.

There must be freedom to inquire so that we can together actually, not theoretically but factually, ensure that you and I have no opinions. This is a tremendous demand because we live on opinions. The media, the newspapers, magazines and books are based on opinions: somebody says something, you agree and that becomes your opinion too; someone else reads a book and forms a different opinion. So to find out the true meaning of peace, and the depth, beauty and quality of it, there must be no bias. Obviously, that is the first demand, not to have faith in peace, or make it the goal of your life to live peacefully, or to get what peace is from books or from others, but to inquire very deeply whether your whole being can live in peace.

Action is not separate from perception. When you see something to be true, that very perception is action. It is not that you perceive and then act because then it is an intellectual concept and you act from that concept. The seeing is the acting — seeing that the world is broken up into tribalism: the British, the Germans, the French, the Americans, the Russians, are all tribes. See the fact that they are tribes, glorified as nations, and that this tribalism is creating havoc, bringing war to the world. Each tribe thinks its own culture differs from others, but tribalism is the root, not the culture. So, observing that fact is the act that frees the brain from the conditioning of tribalism. Are we clear about that? You see, not theoretically or ideationally but as a fact, that tribalism — which has had certain benefits – the very fact that it exists now in the form of glorified nations, is one of the causes of war. That is a fact. There are other causes of war, economics and so on, but one of the causes is tribalism. When you see that this cannot bring about peace, the very perception frees the brain from its tribal conditioning.

Are we together in this? I am not persuading, not trying to convince you of anything. This is not propaganda of any kind but we are facing things as they are, head-on.

One of the factors of contention throughout the world is religion. You are a Christian, I am a Muslim, and so on. Based on ideas, the propaganda of two thousand years – and in the case of Hindus and Buddhists, three to five thousand years – we have been programmed like computers. Please see the fact that this programming has brought about great architecture, great pictures, great chants, great music, but has not brought peace to humanity. When you see that fact, you do not belong to any religion – you are neither a Hindu, a Buddhist nor a Christian – nothing. Spiritual leaders and gurus bring about conflict, contradiction and misery. 'My guru is better than yours, my sect is more sanctified, I have been initiated, you have not' – you know all the nonsense that goes on. So when you see all this as an actual fact all around you,

you do not adhere to any religion, any ideology, any movement, any guru.

Please, this is very serious. If you really want to live peacefully, there must be freedom from all this because these are the causes of dissension and division.

Truth is not yours or mine – that is a fallacy. It doesn't belong to any Church, to any group, to any religion. And peace can exist only when there is freedom from this fallacy. The brain must be free to discover truth. Are we together so far, even intellectually? You know, for most of us to be so drastic about things is very difficult, because we have attributed security to illusions, to things that are not facts, and it is hard to let them go. It is not a matter of using will, just deciding or saying, 'I will not belong to anything.' That is another fallacy. We commit ourselves to something, to a group, to an idea, to religious quackery because we think there is some kind of security in it. But there is no security in any of these things, and therefore no peace. The brain must be secure, but the brain has sought security through thought in things that are illusory. You must be free of that. Can you do it? Are you serious enough to want, crave, demand that you must live in peace? Or right now, perhaps persuaded by me, you say, 'Yes, I understand all that, but . . .' – but, but, but!

What we are doing is talking this over together as two friends. We are friends, you and I; we are two friends who are not persuading or dissuading, not asking each other to commit to something or other – then they would not be friends. We are two friends asking each other whether it is possible to live peacefully for the entire existence of your life. Not at odd moments, not when you have nothing to do, but to live without a single conflict, a single problem.

Let us talk about the brain. I am not a specialist, but I have discussed the brain with many scientists. However, don't accept what the scientists say either; it is far more important to discover for yourself how your brain acts than to be told by scientists what the brain is. The instrument of the brain, with its thought, has not brought about peace in the world or in oneself. That, again, is a fact. And thought has reached the end of its tether.

Where do you explore? And we must be very clear about who is the explorer and what is being explored. If I am exploring what inward peace is, then the 'I' is separate from what is being explored, and so there is division. Where there is division in the inquiry itself, there must be conflict. Please, this is not an intellectual game. To find out the depth and significance of peace, its ramifications, its extent, we must from the outset understand that the explorer is the explored. The explorer is not different from the thing explored. This is difficult for most of us to accept because our conditioning is so strong. This division exists from childhood – the observer and the observed, the examiner and the examined, the investigator who thinks he is separate from what he is investigating. This is our conditioning; it is so; this is a fact. And so we live in perpetual conflict because wherever there is division inwardly or outwardly, there must be conflict. If you like living in conflict, that is your affair. Have a good time, enjoy it, the fun and pain of it, but if you want to discover how to live peacefully, you must understand the basic fact that the explorer is exploring himself, not something outside himself. He is exploring his own structure, own activities, own movements of thought, his own memories – he is all that.

I wonder if you have ever observed that you are a movement of memory, of the faculty for remembering, the faculty of time. An incident might have happened fifty years ago or yesterday, but the faculty for remembering it is memory. And we live on memory – a movement changing, reacting, constantly shaping itself. *We are that*. I wonder if you realise it. But we think progress is the expansion, continuation, the summation of memory, like a computer.

I do not know if you have gone into the challenge that the computer represents – some of you may have. It is rather interesting. Computers are programmed to store countless memories on a single chip. The computer is doing extraordinary things such as designing and building cars. Each generation of computers is better than the previous one. They may not write poems yet but in time they probably will. They may not compose the music of Beethoven but probably they will do some music very well. So, with the advent of the computer, what is going to happen to your brain? Please consider this seriously. This is not blaming anyone but we have talked about this to designers of computers and the progress they have made, and they do not bother about what is going to happen to the human brain; they are concerned solely with the performance of the computer.

We have said that memory is the faculty for remembering things that have happened before – which is necessary technologically and physically. And we have discovered that we are a movement in time, which is the movement of memory. Now, does peace lie in memories?

I can remember days or nights when I saw the extraordinary depth and beauty of peace. That perception, that awareness for a minute, has gone, but I remember

17

it. What is remembered is non-fact, and so we are living in memories that are dead, gone, finished. Please, this is not a depressing or absurd thing for you to turn your back on, but see what memory does to us. Memory accounts for my being programmed as a Hindu, with all that silly nonsense, thinking my culture is better than any other culture because it is thousands of years old; I take great pride in it. So, you are conditioned as I am conditioned – if I am. Which means conditioned by memory – by non-fact – and so I stick to my memories, which are dead things, and you stick to yours – as a Christian, Hindu, Muslim or God knows what.

Of course, we must have memories – you cannot go from here to your home without memory. If you drive a car, you must have memory; if you work in technology you must have an excellent memory to keep your job. But we are talking about memories of pleasant or unpleasant, painful or delightful experiences – the psychological ones. So memories are the conditioning factor. Please see the fact of it, not my explanation of the fact. One of our difficulties is that we like explanations rather than facts – to know, for example, why certain governments are behaving as they do. The journalists and experts explain and we accept the explanation, the logic, the reasons and so on. The description is not the fact. The painting of a mountain, however beautiful, is not the mountain. Some of the pictures in galleries are extraordinarily beautiful but they are not what they depict, which is something that has been seen. You read a novel and it is good literature – if it is – with all the imaginings, romantic business, sex and so on, written by an excellent, well-known author. Again, that is not your life. Your life is here. So, let us find out how to live in peace – but not by a method or system: 'How?' is a wrong question.

Let us go into it. What is the cause of conflict? All of us have conflicts – what is the root of it? What is the root of all problems, whether a religious problem, a problem with meditation, a problem of relationship or a political problem? The root meaning of the word is something thrown, probably hurled, at you. A problem is a challenge. If you respond to a problem with your memories, you will not solve it because your memories are dead, not alive. Do you see the significance of this, that we live with dead things? Our brain is never clear; it is always functioning within the field of memory. And to live with a sense of great abundance, of flowing peace, there must be freedom from the past, from memory. Not memory of how to get to your home or to speak a language – if I had no memory of English, I couldn't talk to you now and you couldn't understand what this poor chap is telling you . . . And I wonder if you do understand what I am telling you!

What is the function of the brain? We can see that one of its major functions is to arrange matters in the physical world. But that very same brain has brought about chaos in the world. The root and source of thought in the brain is the instrument with which we operate. That is a major function of the brain, and that function has created extraordinary trouble and disorder in the world. Yet that same brain has also brought about rapid communications, medicine, great surgery and all the rest of it. Technology is advancing at a tremendous speed, and that very technology is creating havoc in the world with the threat of the atom bomb. Two great powers – I don't know why they are called great powers, they are two idiotic powers – are discussing how to kill each other with the latest missiles. That is what thought has done, being one of the faculties of the brain. Thought has also created the marvellous cathedrals and all the things inside them, which are not therefore God-given or anything supernatural. All the raiment and trappings of the priests are the result of thought, copying the ancient Egyptians.

So, see what thought is doing in the world. Our brain, which has evolved through time, generation after generation, that brain is creating and destroying.

And we accept this way of living. We have never challenged ourselves to find out why we accept this. We have never asked ourselves why we live the way we do in this chaotic world, outwardly and inwardly. We never realise that to have order in the world, there must be order in us. Our own house is the most important thing to clean up first, not the world around us. Some things in it are necessary, like an organisation to stop the killing of whales, to protect nature, rather than destroying the earth searching for more and more oil – you know what is happening, due to rotten governments, for which we are all responsible.

So, what is the deep, fundamental function of the brain? Ask yourself this question. If you ask yourself this, not depending on what others say, their ideas, suppositions and theories, and you begin to inquire very deeply into its fundamental activity, its essence, what is it doing, then what does it want? Is it just survival? Is it just to live in perpetual conflict, division, quarrelling? Is it just to act and function within its own conditioning? Is it just to live perpetually in illusions, and therefore always slightly neurotic, unbalanced, as most people are? If it is none of these things – and obviously it is not – then what is its function? Please, we are asking this question of ourselves. I am not putting the question to you so that you wait

21

for its answer. We will go into it very deeply, but you cannot wait for it to tell you – then it is like . . . then it is nothing; it is as good as any other idea. Or do you really want to find out for yourself the deep function of the brain, and whether the brain is different from the mind, or whether they are the same? When the brain is thoroughly, completely unconditioned, can the mind then act upon the brain? We will go into all this. We have to be very clear where the brain is necessary. Physical activity must exist, in technology, earning a livelihood and so forth. There it must act, and that is one of its great activities. We are going to find out if the brain can be unconditioned.

We were talking the other day to some scientists and doctors – how many experts there are in the world! I am thankful I'm not one of them, just an ordinary person. We were discussing in New York whether the brain cells which are conditioned can mutate in themselves, not by external means but in daily living. If not, we are condemned for ever to live in our conditioning, and therefore in perpetual conflict, with no peace at all.

We must stop now but we will go on to explore the deep function of the brain.

CHAPTER 2

WHAT IS THE DEEP FUNCTION OF THE BRAIN? OBVIOUSLY NOT TO LIVE IN CONFLICT.

We were talking about peace – why human beings, who have lived on this earth for many thousands of years, have had no peace at all. There have been innumerable wars, and there will probably be more. In spite of all the technology we have acquired, and all the protestations of religions about peace, why are we never peaceful, either outwardly in the world or inwardly? The world we have created, and the societies in which we live, are put together by all of us, by the past generations, and will continue to be formed by future generations. We live in a very dangerous, uncertain, insecure world, and there seems to be no peace on earth – why?

We have gone into that, exploring why human beings, who apparently are so clever, so intelligent – which I rather doubt – have failed to create a world we can all live in peacefully. And talking this over together, we came to a particular question: What is the basic function of the brain? That is where we left off. Why the brain, which has evolved for millennia upon millennia, and has had tremendous experiences of every kind – sorrow, pleasure, uncertainty, death – why such a brain has not solved this problem. And who is going to solve it? New leaders, new statesmen, new priests, a new ideology? We have tried all that. Man has tried everything to bring about peace in the world and in himself. And the brain, which is a highly complex organ, capable of extraordinary technological progress, has become very primitive and failed to solve any of its problems.

What is the function of the brain? Just to go on living like this? Acquiring great knowledge in every field and using knowledge to destroy one another, destroy the earth and nature? I hope we are people who are taking life seriously, not casually, and who inevitably ask this. Most of us are only concerned with ourselves, if we are frank and honest. We are concerned with our self-interest, whether we are highly educated intellectuals or uneducated people. The sophisticated or religious among us may identify themselves with something noble, but that very identification is part of self-interest. And the brain, our brain, is concerned with that – with personal problems, mathematical problems, technological problems. We are basically concerned with ourselves. That is a fact. However much we may try to hide self-interest in noble work, in meditation, in belonging to various groups, consciously or unconsciously self-interest dominates. If we are honest and look into ourselves and our political and religious activities, and so on, we see we are basically self-concerned. We have lived that way from the beginning of time and are still doing so. And the brain is therefore functioning only in a very small, limited field.

So, is that the function of the brain, to be concerned with itself, its problems, its pleasures and sorrows, pain, ambition, greed and so on, with the resulting chaos in the world? Each one wants to fulfil, to achieve, to become enlightened or become a big businessman – which is the same thing. We have reduced our brain, which is an extraordinary instrument, to something petty and very limited. It can be extraordinarily successful technologically, producing weapons, surgical instruments, medicines, communications and computers – there the brain has functioned with extraordinary vitality and capacity – and yet that very brain is concerned with its own self-protective activity.

The brain is living on memories, not on facts. This is very important to understand if we are going to explore how the brain works, and the quality of a brain that can penetrate and find its deep function. We are dealing only with facts, and the fact is that we are a series of movements of memory – as we talked about the other day. Memory, which has nothing to do with facts, has become extraordinarily important. My father is dead, he is gone, and I remember. There is remembrance and I live on, cherish the memories of the incidents we shared together. So, we are a series of movements of memory and time. Memory is time. Memory is the reaction of experience, knowledge and the things that you remember. This is what the self is, what we are.

I do not know if you have ever inquired into what the present, what the 'now' is. Is it the cessation of memory? Or we just don't know what the 'now' is at all? May I go into it a little bit? Zero was invented by the ancient Hindus, and in zero all the numbers are contained. Is the 'now' the totality of all time? We have seen that the brain has cultivated self-interest, accumulated memories, and has become a very minor psychological instrument. When I am thinking about myself all day long, it is a very small affair. Or even when I think about the whole world, it is still a small affair.

So why has the brain got caught in this narrow circle of the self? The self, the 'me', the ego, all that, is nothing but words and memories. That self has become terribly important, and when you are self-concerned, all your actions must be psychologically limited. Where there is limitation, there must be conflict. I am a Jew, you are an Arab – that is a limitation, limited tribalism, and I cling to my limitation and you cling to yours, and so there is perpetual conflict. If you are constantly repeating 'I am a Russian,' and identify with that particular country, its tradition, language and literature, it is very limited. The brain seeking security in the self has made itself psychologically limited.

Clearly, there is a contradiction between this psychological limitation and the extraordinarily limitless nature of technological progress. And is it then the function of the brain to live in perpetual conflict and contradiction, never being free from this, just functioning in a small psychological area? Is it possible to break this limitation down when you understand the nature of the self? But who is to break it down? This limitation has been brought about by thought, which has sought security in limitation, and thought itself is limited because it is the outcome of experience and accumulated knowledge stored in the brain cells. I am not an expert but have watched very carefully. Thought is the outcome of memory that is limited, knowledge that will always be limited, and experience that is never complete. Do you see this?

So the brain functions with limited thought as its instrument. Therefore we are living in perpetual conflict, struggle, pain and sorrow, because we seek security in this limitation, in memories. Is it the brain's function to seek security in order to ensure physical survival? You must of course seek to survive physically, but you seek not only physical but also psychological security – and is there psychological security at all? Don't, please, accept what is being said; go into it very carefully. Together we are examining, not imposing, not trying to convince you of anything. I really mean this. We are not trying to convert you to a philosophy, which is a horror. Let it be as though we are walking together down a shady lane full of dappled light, with the beauty of the earth around us. And we are talking about serious issues, not petty things, because we are both serious. And we are asking: Is this what we have reduced our life to, just seeking self-security in limitation? We have no physical security because of war, because of racial, tribal, ideological conflict. The politicians are preparing for war – you know all that. And you cannot talk to politicians; they won't listen because they are anxious to preserve their own position – you know all that. So we are asking: Is it the only function of the brain to seek security in limitation? That is what we are doing. And in searching for security in limitation we are bringing about havoc in the world, great disorder and confusion.

Now, what is the function of thought? That is the instrument of the brain. What is thought? What is thinking? We all think, whether we are highly educated, sophisticated, or an uneducated person with little food and shelter. Thinking is common to an educated person who can express things clearly, and someone who cannot. So thinking is common to all of us — it is not *your* thinking. You may express it differently, you may be an artist, a mathematician or a biologist, and I may be a layman, but we both think. So thinking is not yours. Please, this is a fundamental thing to understand. Thinking is not individual, and yet we say, 'This is what I think. This is my opinion, my judgement. These are my values.' See what is happening to us: we have reduced the whole vast process of thinking down to *mine*.

We ought also to inquire if your brain is separate from another's. We will go into this slowly. Please don't get impatient or cling to your own particular view. The brain has evolved in time, through thousands of years of experience, knowledge and all the activities of thought in the world — technological, personal. All that thinking! And we say, 'It is my brain that I think with.' But is that so? Is it yours? It is the result of millions of years of evolution, so it is not your brain or my brain, it is *brain*. I wonder if you see the depth of this. And the brain is the centre of our consciousness.

What is our consciousness? If you ask yourself that question, you see it is your beliefs, conclusions, opinions, two thousand years of being programmed. Your consciousness is the reactions, reflexes, fears, pleasures, sorrows, pain, grief and all the misery of human beings. That is your consciousness. Is your consciousness different from another's, or is it like the consciousness of all humanity? They suffer in Russia, India, China. They may wear different clothing, the environment may be different, but psychologically the content of our consciousness is common to all human beings. Your brain and consciousness are shared by all human beings, so you are like the rest of humanity. You may be German, Swiss or a proud Englishman, but you are like the rest of humanity. Now, this is not an intellectual concept, an idea, a romantic, sentimental something – it is a fact. And when that is deeply real, when that is the truth, then your whole outlook on life changes. Then you are responsible for all humanity. It is rather frightening but it is so. Therefore, you need to understand that in our investigation we are not being self-centred, we are not cultivating the self, making the self more intelligent, but we are seeing that we are like the rest of mankind. Out of that comes compassion.

Is the brain an instrument that is merely concerned with security – psychological as well as physical security? If it is not, then what is the function of the brain? If I am not everlastingly concerned with myself in my meditation – you know, all that silly stuff – then what place has thought? Is there a new instrument altogether that is not the activity of thought? We can see what thought has done technologically: it has produced the most extraordinarily beautiful things – architecture, paintings, marvellous poems, great novels – but thought has also divided people. It has, through that divisiveness, created wars. So thought is not the instrument of peace. I wonder if this is clear. Are we meeting each other, walking together? Thought, being in itself divisive and limited, cannot possibly bring about peace in the world. This is clearly shown by the League of Nations, the United Nations, Napoleon or Hitler trying to conquer Europe and so on. So, the activity of thought cannot possibly resolve human problems. If you see that very clearly, then what?

I see very clearly what thought has done in the world and I see very clearly what thought has done in

31

the realm of my own psyche. The search for security is the basis of the movement of thought, but is there security at all through thought? Or is there security only when thought, with its own intelligence and cunning, realises its place and does not enter into the area of the psyche? Are we together in this? I will go into it a little more.

Life is a movement in relationship; we cannot live by ourselves. In that relationship are innumerable problems: sexual problems, psychological problems, the problems of companionship and loneliness – the whole problem of relationship. What is relationship? When you are related to your wife or husband, your father or mother, and so on, when you say, 'I am related,' what does that word *related* mean? Not its dictionary meaning, which we all know, but the depth, the significance of the word. I am related to my wife, and in this relationship there is perpetual conflict – which you probably know more about than I do. Why this conflict? When we ask that question, we are trying to find out if this conflict can end. *End*. And to find out whether it can end, we must face the actual fact of what our relationship is to another, however intimate it may be.

Is our relationship based on thought? Please, I am asking you this question but you have to put it to yourself. We are two friends talking over things together. One friend asks the other: Why is there conflict in our relationship? Is our relationship based on pleasant or unpleasant incidents, which are remembered, and each of us lives on those memories, which is thought? I am ambitious and so is she. She wants to fulfil in her way and I want to fulfil in mine. She has come to definite conclusions and so have I. So there is always a division, and where there is division there must be conflict. This is simple.

To understand the nature of conflict and see whether it is possible to end conflict in relationship, we have to inquire whether thought dominates the relationship and ask whether thought is love. Don't respond, please – this is much too serious to agree or disagree with. Go into it for yourself. It is the activity of thought in relationship that has bound us together through memory, through reactions, through pleasure, sexual and otherwise. So thought is *the* factor in relationship. She has said something that has hurt me and I have hurt her in return. That hurt is being carried on, which is memory. It is like two parallel lines never meeting, and this we call relationship. Whether with a woman or man, a political leader, priest or guru, it is all based on thought and memory. So, is remembrance the activity of love? Please ask this. If it is, we are living on dead memories. Memories are the past, the capacity to remember.

Now, is there a way of living without conflict in relationship? Is there a way of living in relationship with another into which memory doesn't enter, without the accumulation of memory about the other? This is the ending of thought. And is love the activity of thought? You may ask these questions, but merely asking them does not provide the solution.

To find out how to live in this world peacefully, we have to understand the depth and nature of thought and memory. Most of us from early childhood bear the burden of many hurts and psychological wounds, the memory of these hurts and their continued effects. Can all that be wiped away? If I am hurt, how can I love another? Please, this is not a sermon, it is real inquiry so that you begin to see directly for yourself that conflict can end. And that possibility exists only and truly when you have inquired deeply into the whole nature of the self and into self-interest, which is based on reward and punishment. Then you begin to find out for yourself that thought is not the instrument to solve human problems. Even with technological problems, you may think a great deal, work things out, but there too you only discover something new when thought is in abeyance. If you remain in the field of knowledge all the time, there is nothing new.

Will inquiring whether the brain can live in peace affect society? It may not. But we are not seeking an effect. If each one of us sees the activity of thought, its limitation, and the activities of memory, and therefore the very divisive result and consequent conflict, if you actually see the truth of that and live it, then you might ask what effect this has on society as a whole. Perhaps none! Does it matter? Are you concerned with changing society, making it more orderly? Actually, if you face the fact, you really aren't. But if I may point out, it is a wrong question to ask what effect a fundamental mutation in my brain has on society. The truth of that fundamental mutation will act, not you.

I don't know if you have ever wondered what intelligence is. What is intelligence? It is a very complicated question. How do you receive that question, how do you approach it? Our brain is trained from childhood to solve problems – mathematical, historical and so on, through exams. Our brain is trained to solve architectural problems, engineering problems, how to build a motor. This means we approach life itself with a brain that is trying to solve problems. I don't know if you realise this. You treat life as a problem and then try to find a solution to it. So when I ask you a question like 'What is intelligence?' you make that into a problem, naturally. And then you try to solve it with a brain that is trained in problem-solving. Can you look at this question not as a problem? If you do, it is the beginning of intelligence. That means the brain is already becoming free from its conditioning. But if you approach the question trying to solve it, you are back in the old muddle. When you realise that your brain is conditioned to solve problems, and you therefore approach any question with a brain that says, 'I must solve it,' you see that you will never meet its challenge afresh. To meet any problem afresh is the beginning of intelligence.

We started out by asking whether humanity can live in peace, because if it cannot live in peace we cannot flower and life becomes terribly small and petty. In this inquiry, we see that you and I are like the rest of the world, like the rest of humanity, whether you like it or not. You may stick to your conditioning that you are a separate individual, but you are not. You may have a different body, a different name, be a different colour, you may have long hair or short hair, you may speak German or Russian, but you stand on the same ground as the rest of humanity.

And we said that the brain has its function, and what is the root, the basis of that function? Obviously not to live in conflict. When that is put to you, you say 'Yes, I must solve that. But how?' Then you get the systems, methods, arguments, the pros and cons and all the rest of it. But when the brain is not approaching that question, that challenge, with its old, trained condition, then you can look at it totally anew, afresh. Isn't that the capacity of intelligence, to look at something clearly and not try to solve it?

We will explore further whether there is a possibility of finding something totally new that is not the activity of thought.

CHAPTER 3

THE SELF, IN ITS ISOLATING STATE,
SEEKS SECURITY IN ILLUSIONS.

Shall we continue with what we were talking about? I must make the serious point that you will not be getting help from me. There is no help outside ourselves. It has to be clearly understood that no political or religious authority, or any kind of guru with their systems and theories trying to help people or do good, has succeeded – we have had all that for thousands of years. There is no help from outside. If I may use the Christian word, there is no *salvation* outside, through anybody, any theological or political system. I have to rely completely on myself, be totally responsible for myself – what I do, what I think – and not put the blame on others, on the environment, on heredity or on my genes. We have played endlessly with all that in various ways, pursued every kind of philosophy and put great faith in something or other, always something *outside* – a symbol, a person, a conclusion, an idea. All these have failed because after millennia we are what we are now. And it is not just the past generations that have produced this chaos – they have helped and we are adding to it.

Please bear in mind that we are not relying on any book, theory, symbol or person, including myself. I am not excluding myself because you have to be very careful not to be influenced or stimulated by me, not rely on me to make things clear. It has to be absolutely, fundamentally clear that there is no outside help to discover what we are, what human beings have become after all these centuries of evolution – brutal, violent, the whole business. You cannot blame it on anyone, or go back to the past and try to find out the causes. There are multiple causes and we can quarrel over these endlessly. But the fact remains: we are what we are now, after thousands of years of evolution.

We are talking this over as two friends. Being friends, we can talk without seeking to influence or dominate each other. As friends who have known each other for some time, we are discussing the human problem because that is far more important than any technological problem. Unless psychological problems are resolved, they will always overwhelm the technological. You may have marvellous technology, the realm of the computer, but the human psyche overcomes the computer. The computer may give a set of good instructions – that you should do this or that, but the psyche in each one of us can transcend and do what it wants in spite of it. I think this is very clear.

So, please, we must start with doubt, with a certain quality of scepticism that questions everything in human existence, apart from the physical aspect. You cannot doubt a surgeon if he says you have cancer. You may try to, but if several doctors tell you you've got it, you accept it and stop doubting. You can try various cures, and all the quacks in the world will rush to you, but eventually you have to accept what the doctors say. But the psychological world is much more complex; it needs acute sensitivity to its great intricacies, its subtleties, and that demands a brain that is very clear, not confused or self-centred. You cannot examine or look at the whole complexity of self-promotion unless you are critical of it; unless you are questioning, doubting, asking. But the present religion in the West denies any questioning or doubting: you must not doubt, you must have faith – and so the quality of doubt, which is so vital to human existence, is denied. Whereas in Buddhism and Hinduism, doubt has been one of the pillars of inquiry.

By reading some book or other, you think it will do you good. You must be very clear that you have to be a light to yourself, which does not mean self-assertiveness or tremendous self-confidence. It does not mean pursuing one's desires and fulfilment. To be a light to yourself means standing totally alone psychologically. The word *alone*, from Latin, Greek and so on, means all one, together, whole, not fragmented. But we misinterpret that aloneness as isolation. We are afraid of being isolated and don't understand the meaning and depth of the state of being alone.

Doubt what I am saying and doubt your own reactions to it. Have doubt, the seed of doubt; not what you doubt but the seed. Let it move, flower, grow until it finds the truth. And be alone to inquire, to find out the truth of that statement. Not just hearing and accepting the words but discovering their depth for yourself. I hope we are together on this.

As we said, we have sought security in the things of thought, that which thought has put together, which means your family, the community, the larger community and so on. We have sought security in isolation, security in the nation, in belonging to something, to this or that group, belonging or not belonging to a Church. We have sought security in all that. And you discover for yourself that there is no security in isolation. Now, is that a fact or is it just a theory? Do you see the distinction? If it is a theory, there are theories galore, but if you examine your own desire to be secure, you will find, if you go into it, that you have sought security in isolation. The isolation may be extensive in range but it is still isolation. And this process of isolation is fragmentation. Where there is the pursuit of security in isolation, as in the Arab or the Jew, the seeking of security in that isolation is fragmentation. And then the problem arises: How can the fragments ever be brought together? That is a wrong question because the cause of the fragments is the search for security in isolation. If you are free of that cause, there is no fragmenting and therefore no searching for security in isolation, either in the family or self-centred isolation.

See what is actually happening in the world. I am asking you, my friend, to look very closely at that. The family, the community, the larger community, the nation – these are isolating processes. In national isolation, there is a search for supreme political and religious power – this whole sense of gaining power. And so there is more and more confusion, more and more destruction, there are more and more problems. This is very clear if you go into it, not casually, not by reading books but by seeing the fact of it in yourself. You have to inquire further to find out why we seek security. Not that we should not have it physically. For the baby to grow up there must be security; for human beings to live happily for at least a while, they must have security, food, clothes, a dwelling. But the process of isolation is denying that to everybody. Each government is concerned with itself, with its own economy and people. Saving its own people by war, not other peoples. I heard the other day a general saying, 'I do not like killing people but we have to because primarily we must save our own people.' And they are trained to do that. Do you see the enormous significance, the fact, the truth, that in isolation there is never security, no security at all? It is very difficult to break down the state of the brain that has been conditioned, taught, educated to seek to fulfil itself in isolation.

Now, what is security apart from physical security? What is it to be secure? Please ask this. We are doing it as two friends sitting together in a quiet room, overlooking a pleasant valley on a lovely morning, asking each other seriously what security is, what it means to be secure. Is there security in relationship? Ask yourself that. We want security in relationship, thinking that this implies trust, confidence, love, all that. And yet while we want security in one another, each of us is pursuing his or her own isolation, his or her own self-centred activity. We want the security of a peaceful life, not to have any conflict, not to have any bother, any problems, just to live – and that is not happening either. So, what is security and where do we find it? Not in some theory, not in some image that thought has projected and made holy, not in any symbol made by thought.

Where do you find total, complete security? The brain needs security, but at present the brain is confused. A philosopher says this, a scientist says that, a guru or Church says something else, and so on. After thousands of years of this, the brain is actually confused, and in that confusion says, 'I must be secure.' It then invents a new illusion. Do you see what goes on? I have dropped this illusion because I find no security in it, then I succumb to another one and hope to find security in that. This is what we are doing. So where do you find security? Unless the brain is completely secure, completely certain, unconfused, it must be in turmoil. And if you examine your own life, your own existence, my friend, you will see how confused you are, how uncertain – you cannot rely on anything. So where do you find security? Not outwardly, obviously. And will you find security in the psyche, in the 'me', in the self? Don't say, 'No' – let's find out.

Which leads to the next question: What is the self, what is the 'me', the whole psychological structure?

What is the 'me'? Is the 'me' a series of conclusions? It is. I believe. I am convinced. I have faith, I am this or that – you can expand it. So, if security is not to be found outside, is it possible to find it inwardly? Please ask this. I hope to find it within me, somewhere inwardly, which means I must have more confidence in myself – that is how we translate it. What does confidence in myself mean? In my experience, in my knowledge, in my prayers? All of which is the 'me', put together by thought – I have faith in something, I believe in something, I belong to something. All that, surely, is the movement of thought. Thought has created the mess outside, the confusion, the terrible things that are happening in the world, and thought has also created the 'me'. It was not some kind of divine explosion that created 'me'. From childhood I have been taught, educated, trained, and that 'me' comes first. So, we are examining whether there is security in the 'me'. And the 'me' is put together by thought. We must be very clear on this.

When I say I believe in and have faith in God, when I say that my security is in God, who has created that God? Please be factual. Don't think I'm attacking. I am not attacking, my friend – that would be too silly.

And he is not attacking me either. Nor are we being defensive, resisting each other, but together we are questioning, doubting, asking. My friend says, 'You have faith in God,' and I say, 'Perhaps I do.' And being friends, we discuss it. Instead of saying, 'I believe,' or 'I don't believe, and I am going to stick to that,' we say, 'Who created this idea of God?' Then my friend asks, 'But how did all human existence come into being?' And the scientific answer is more reasonable than all the theories and speculations, the belief in God and so on. Coming from the ocean, we have taken four, five, ten million years to evolve to the present state. It has taken time to bring about a human being.

So, my friend says to me, look carefully at what your thought has created. Seeking security, being frightened of death and so on, you have created or thought has created something which you then worship, try to find security in, in contrast to what you are doing, in contrast to your life. I may believe in the most extraordinary things like God – the supreme intelligence, you know, the highest principle – but it has to be a reality in my life, otherwise it is of no value. Please, I am not advocating atheism. We are questioning each other on this fundamental issue, which is the urge and demand, the necessity for security. And we find we have sought security in illusions.

Now, what next? Please look at it carefully. If you see something to be actually, factually false, and yet hold onto that, you are not being intelligent. My friend says, 'This is not actual, this is just an invention.' And in that kind of inventiveness, illusion in romantic, sentimental nonsense, there is no security. So please see the false as the false. Which means you have already discovered what is true. I see something false, I see an illusion as an illusion. The English word *illusion* means a plaything, from the Latin *ludere,* something not real. So my friend says, 'You live with fallacies.' And when I see they are fallacies, what has happened to my brain?

The brain has accepted for centuries something that is not actual: the vast majority of mankind believes in God because God is their security. Whereas God is an invention. When I see that, the conditioning of the brain is broken down. Do you see it? I have been going north all my life and you come along and say north is an illusion. As we are friends, we talk this over and I say, 'By Jove, that is right,' and turn and go east. Which means what? I have broken the system, the habit, the conditioning of the brain, which has been going in one direction. Suddenly it breaks away from this and goes in another direction. There is a breaking of the conditioning. The habit has been broken of pursuing an illusion, and the brain cells have therefore changed. The very cells have changed because the brain had pursued a habit and has broken it – not through enforcement, not through will or through any action, but through pure logic, sanity and seeing the fact.

So where is security? We have to find out whether there is complete security or not. We have to be very clear about the process of thought. I will go into it again.

Thought is a limited process, a materialistic process, because thought is based on experience – sensory, reactive, reflective experience. And from that limited experience knowledge is formed. So knowledge is always limited, whether scientific or psychological. This is so. It is so simple. And so memory is limited because it is based on time, the duration of time. And thought is limited because there is no thought without memory. So whatever it does is limited. Your prayers are limited; all the things in the church are limited, put together by thought. Are you resisting this? I know why you are resisting it – you are frightened, you might lose your job.

We were talking the other day to a priest, having a good, friendly discussion. He said, 'I agree with you, but how am I to live?' This applies to most of us as well. Please understand this very simple fact, that where there is the limited activity of thought, whatever it does in the world, there must be conflict. If I keep on repeating, 'I am a Christian,' 'I am a Buddhist,' I am this, I am that, it is very limited, and that very limitation must bring about conflict. And in conflict, there is no security. Unless you love conflict and say it is part of your being . . . Well, all right, then that means . . . there is a hole in your head!

When you see something as false, when you see the limited activities of thought and its conflicts, you abandon the false. You don't just say, 'Yes I see the false as the false,' and leave it at that. When you see that which is not true, not actual, that which is false, illusory, it is the ending of that illusion. Not that you conclude it to be so, but the very seeing of the fact is the ending of the illusion. What happens then to the brain that was conditioned by the false? There is a mutation in the brain cells themselves. Suppose I have a very strong habit. When I break a habit, when there is seeing its futility, there is the ending of it, and therefore a change in the very structure of the brain. So what has taken place when I see that which is false as false and there is the ending of that? If you do it as we go along, my friend, then what has taken place? Please find out. Hasn't the brain become clear? It has cast off burdens that are false. Seeing that which is false, seeing is acting. So, what has happened to the brain that sees?

We will approach it differently. Most of us want to become something. In the physical world, we want to be someone. I am a clerk in a big corporation and gradually I work my way up. If I am good, capable, I become a manager. From a manager, I step higher until I become an executive, and then the president. Through time I have become the president. This is a physical process. We then carry the same movement over into the psychological realm. I am this but I will become that. It is the same movement, in no way different. Both require time, time to become. What is becoming? I can understand it in the physical world: I earn more money, have a better car, better house, more paintings – if I have money, I buy a Rembrandt, or I drink more – you know, the whole business of modern culture. I become something in the material world, and I extend that same movement to becoming something in the religious area. One day I will become enlightened, reach the highest principle, God or whatever you call it. By righteous behaviour, step by step I will become something. That is the whole system of religious thought. I go to the guru and the silly guru teaches me. I will one day become like him, which means having power and disciples.

Follow all this very carefully. I ask my friend: What is it that is becoming? When I say I will gradually experience enlightenment, gradually build up to it, what does that mean? Is there a becoming? Question that. Not that I shouldn't become something psychologically, but we must put the question: Is there anything to become? Is it my self, my experience, my memories, my projection of what I should be? That means I must have time for all this. And we are saying quite the contrary. It has been said that to become wise or enlightened is a process. I am saying to my friend that it sounds nonsensical – like the whole Buddhist concept that the Buddha went through phases until he ultimately reached enlightenment – which I question. Is enlightenment, understanding or perception a matter of time?

What is time? Time is a movement. Time to go from here to your home. It is a movement in time, to cover distance. You need to have physical time to go from here to your home. That is time. And to become something requires time. In the physical world, you have set a goal for yourself to become the manager and you require time, and you have also set a goal to become something psychologically. For example, to become non-violent. We are violent, and it is said that to become non-violent needs time. We are

51

questioning, doubting that. You have to doubt this whole idea of becoming non-violent, which they have preached a great deal. The fact is violence: I am angry, I am jealous, I am furious, I hate somebody, I want to be somebody more powerful. That is a fact, but non-violence is non-fact. So, what am I doing? Pursuing, cultivating a non-fact. And to achieve non-fact requires time. See the absurdity of it! And millions upon millions believe this.

So the fact is I am violent, and to achieve non-fact requires time. But to stay with violence needs no time. To understand, observe, perceive the nature, structure and causation of violence needs no time because it is a fact. If I look at it carefully, it will reveal the whole thing. But if I am pursuing non-violence, I am not observing. So please understand something: perception does not require time. I am violent – what do I mean by that word? Violence can exist only when there is contradiction in me, when there are two separate activities contradicting each other. I say one thing and do another, think one thing and act totally differently. That is a contradiction, which creates opposites. So I have discovered something: where there is contradiction, opposites, there must be conflict. That conflict indicates violence. Comparison, imitation and conformity are essentially violence. When I compare myself with you who are much brighter, I am antagonistic to you, jealous of you. Jealousy, conformity and antagonism are violence. When I put away the non-real – non-violence – I see very clearly all the intimations and complexity of violence. When there is a perception of this, there is the ending of it. That violence is not separate from me.

When you are angry, is anger different from you? When you are sexually excited, is that excitement different from you? So is violence or comparison different from you, or are you all that? We have been trained from childhood to compare. We go to school and are given marks. We are subject to comparison throughout our school life and then at university if we are lucky enough – or unlucky enough. Then when it comes to a job we are still comparing, fighting, struggling. Here we are saying all that is a form of violence, aggression and so on. Now, to see the fact of that, not the non-fact of non-violence but the fact that I am violent, to see the entirety of violence, there is a perception only when the non-fact is completely put aside. When there is no pursuit of non-violence of any kind, the whole of attention is on the fact. Then the fact moves, reveals, shows what it is. And that very perception is the ending of it because there is no conflict due to violence being separate from me. Violence is me, as anger, as are your reactions, as when you have pain in your stomach, or toothache or a headache, it is you. You are not separate from all that. Where there is separation there must be conflict, as the Jew, the Muslim, the Hindu.

So, there is security only in intelligence. It is intelligence that says that something is false because you have examined, looked, doubted, questioned. If you say, 'I accept the false as truth,' then you are unintelligent. But the moment you look at the falseness of things and see clearly the false as the false, that perception is the beginning of intelligence. That intelligence, which we shall go into deeply, is security. Intelligence of that kind is supreme security.

CHAPTER 4

CONFLICT CAUSES DETERIORATION OF THE BRAIN.

We were saying that human beings throughout the world have sought security, and they must have security physically. But they have also sought psychological security and have invented all kinds of images, theories and hypotheses to bring that about. Physical security is obviously necessary; worldwide all of us should have food, clothes and shelter. But that is denied by various forms of division. We have hardly any physical security, and psychologically, inwardly, we have sought security in illusions – in God, in ideas, in relationship, in concepts, prejudices, conclusions, convictions. None of these have given human beings inward security. We are asking: Is there security at all for human beings?

Please kindly bear in mind that this is not a lecture, not a discourse on a particular subject to instruct or inform, nor is it something ideological, philosophical or exotic from the East. We are talking like two friends about human existence, why human beings after countless millennia are still psychologically primitive, while technologically highly advanced. We have been to the moon, invented a great many things, rapid communications, advanced surgery, medicine and computers which may perhaps take over the whole activity of our brain – not quite all, but most of it. And we are asking ourselves why human beings are what they are now, after the prolonged span of time called evolution. Human beings are still violent, brutal, primitive, have international wars, economic wars, and so on. Clearly, there is no peace in the world, and no government, of whatever country, is capable of bringing it about.

Is there any psychological security? We have tried to find it in every form of illusion, in attachment, in ties, and so on, but none of them has provided security, a security that is stable, firm, not fluctuating, not changing, but steady, conveying great strength and vitality. And we have said that only in intelligence is there total security.

Now, we are going to inquire together into the nature of intelligence. According to the dictionary, it means to understand, discern, to grasp quickly a statement, idea or proposal. And to have sagacity, which is to apply the capacity to discern instantly. Each of us when we hear the word *intelligence* will translate it according to our conditioning and prejudices. We say, 'That is an intelligent book,' or 'He is an intelligent man,' meaning someone who has the capacity to investigate, to observe, to think things out. And the root of the word *intelligence* means not only to discern, to capture instantly something that may be new, it also means to read between the lines, between two thoughts. And the very word *intelligence* has an extraordinary sound.

When you hear that word, what does it mean to you? First, we hear the sound of the word. Of course, the word itself is not intelligence. The word is not the thing, but the word has its own verbal significance, and behind the word is its sound. The sound contains the deeper significance of the word. Sound is very important. Music is sound; a rapidly flowing river makes sound. Yet we hardly listen to sound. We have prejudices that not only prevent us from hearing what the word is communicating, but also prevent us from capturing its sound. That means one has to listen very carefully for the word itself to unfold its full significance. And you can listen only when there is the sound that the word brings about. If you listen also to the sound of the words 'beautiful morning', you capture the whole significance of the morning, with all its extraordinary beauty, the shadows, the clear air, the mountains. In the sound of that phrase, all these things exist.

What is intelligence? How do you approach a question like that? Each of us will give a different meaning to it according to our capacity. If you have read a great deal, speak many languages, are gifted in various ways, you would call that intelligence. And someone else might say you must have the capacity to discern without choosing. Another person might say that to put together the whole complex workings of a computer is intelligence. So each, according to their predilection, prejudice, bias and conclusions, will say what intelligence is. But to investigate what intelligence *really* is, we must first negate what it is not. We must identify unintelligence to find out what intelligence is. Through negation, you come to the positive, but if you start with the positive you end up negatively. So, we are starting now to find out what intelligence is not. That is, we are thinking together. It is not that I am telling you, but together we are investigating this enormous and complex problem. And to do that there must first be negation. If we are clear on this, we can proceed.

What is not intelligence? Is war intelligence? All the nastiness, ugliness, brutality, the bloodshed and the killing of people and animals, the whales of the ocean – is that intelligence? We are killing perpetually,

not only nature but ourselves; our brains are degener-
ating. We see war is not intelligent, yet engage in it.
Every one of us is responsible for this but I am not sure
if you would acknowledge such responsibility. There
are wars going on in the world at the present time,
killing each other for ideas and ideals, to assert status
and power as nations, so as not to be encroached upon
or surrounded. Is that the action of intelligence?
Human beings, who have evolved over a long passage
of time, have had two appalling world wars, and yet
are preparing for another. That is obviously an act of
great stupidity. One of its causes is nationalism, which
is glorified tribalism: my country, my space, my
people, my tradition, my God. All such activity is the
action of stupidity, not intelligence. I think you would
all agree to that. But do we see the fact of it, not just
verbally assert that it is stupid?

What is our responsibility – we will get very close
to home now – when you see this going on? If I belong
to a certain tribe with its nationalism, or to a religious
sect that brings about division and therefore conflict, I
either accept that conflict and follow the usual trad-
itional path, or I actually no longer belong to any
country, any tribe, to any group, sect or religion.
Because these are the factors of division and therefore
conflict, and of the deterioration of the brain which is

happening to all of us. Conflict is a major factor in the deterioration of the brain, and human beings from childhood until they die are in perpetual conflict about one thing or another; conflict that comes into being when there is contradiction, when you say one thing and do something totally different. That is hypocrisy. Are you listening now? As friends, are we listening to each other? Or do you say, 'Yes, quite right, I agree,' and then carry on in the same old way?

As we said, this is serious. It is not entertainment, not intellectual stimulation or something romantic or senti-mental and all that nonsense. This is very serious. Not only has life become very dangerous for most people, but life also has apparently no meaning whatsoever. And if we are to take life seriously, which we must if we are intelligent, we must be concerned about all this. Not just one aspect of it, but concerned about the whole of human existence. Not going off into some kind of absurd meditation, following a guru or being tied to some theory or ideal. This is a serious matter, which means exercising your brain to find out for yourself what is true and what is illusory. And nationalism of any kind, bringing about division and war, is obviously not an act of intelligence. When you see something to be true, the false simply drops away. There is no longer conflict, or even determination not to be a nationalist.

Nationalism is one of the factors of conflict, and so too is holding on to prejudice. The word *prejudice* means preconceived opinion. And we are full of prejudices, your opinion versus someone else's. Political opinion is dividing people all over the world. Opinion means a suggestion, lacking proof, based on an emotional reaction, with strong adherence to a conclusion. This divides people and therefore there is conflict. Can we live – please listen, my friend – without opinion and prejudice? After all, it is prejudice when you believe in some kind of god, when as a Christian you very strongly believe in a saviour, and someone else, a Hindu or Buddhist believes something else. Your belief in a saviour is just a matter of belief or faith, without any proof. And your belief has not brought about peace in the world.

When you see all this, how belief, prejudice, conclusions and ideals divide people and therefore breed conflict, you see that such activity is obviously not intelligence. Will you drop all your prejudices, all your opinions about what you are, what you are not, what you should be, and so on? Will you drop all that so that you have a free, uncluttered mind? If you say it is not possible, you will never find out for yourself – we are saying this as a friend – what it is to be intelligent. You will therefore always search for security in an illusion, and then never finding it, be in turmoil, confusion, neuroticism, and escape into sentimentality, romanticism or sensuality. This is what is happening.

So, as we have said, one of the major factors in the deterioration of the brain is this constant division that breeds conflict. Why is there such division in us, such fragmentation? Why is there in all human beings worldwide this contradiction, this fragmentation, and therefore the urge to bring all the fragments together and to fulfil? Let us examine this, because we want to see what intelligence, supreme intelligence really is, not the limited intelligence of thought based on knowledge and experience – because knowledge and experience are limited, and anything limited is not intelligence.

I hope we are meeting each other as would two friends on a trail, stopping to sit down quietly, listening to the birds, the nearby stream, seeing the beautiful, still mountains, and by inquiry establishing not just an intellectual, verbal understanding but establishing in our life the real quality of intelligence.

Why is there in us duality, these opposites? Wanting, not wanting, *what is* and *what should be* – you are greedy, you should not be greedy; you are violent, you should not be violent; you are dull, stupid and conform or imitate and compare your own stupidity with somebody who is not stupid. There is this constant struggle.

I am hoping you won't go to sleep, that you are really interested in this, and pursue it to the end, not just have a casual interest in it. You don't have a casual interest in making money, a casual interest in having sex, a casual interest in having a job. You have to have a job, you have to have money, but this is far more important than a job, sex or anything else because when there is that intelligence, it will operate in all the areas of your life. But unfortunately, we don't carry things through to the very end. That is why we are all mediocre. Forgive me for saying this. The word *mediocre* means going halfway up a hill, never going to the very top. And we are trying to understand, and live, a life of intelligence. To do that you have to see not only what the causes of conflict are but also what brings those causes to an end.

What is a fact and what is not a fact? When there is only fact, the fact has no duality, no opposite. Love has no opposite as hate. The fact is that which has happened and that which is happening now. But we draw a conclusion from what has happened before and hold on to that conclusion. That conclusion is not a fact. What is happening now is a fact, but we never look at the fact; we make an abstraction of it as an idea, and then pursue the idea, which is non-fact. So can we stay only with the fact?

I am envious. That is a fact. Not me personally – I am not envious; I don't care. But suppose we are envious. That is a fact. That is what is taking place, a reaction that we call envy. And out of that fact, we draw a conclusion that we must not be envious, so we pursue the non-fact and create an opposite to *what is*. So, don't pursue the non-fact; remain with the fact. The fact is you are not separate from envy. This is difficult for you to see because we say the 'me' is different from the action, 'me' is different from the reaction, 'me' is different from my envy, my anger and so on. That is what we have been conditioned to. This means we have been conditioned to conflict.

Now somebody comes along and says, 'Only when the brain ceases to deteriorate can the brain be intelligent.' To end that deteriorating factor is to hold on to the fact and put away all non-fact, idealism, conclusion, prejudice. Holding on only to the fact. The fact is we are envious. Now, if you hold on to the fact, what is implied in that? With the alternative, when you pursue non-fact, time is involved. If I pursue non-violence when I am violent, the achieving of non-violence requires time. To become non-violent

64

requires time. Whereas if you remain with the fact, no time is involved.

Time is a movement of thought, psychologically as well as physically. Time is not only the past, the future and the present but the whole movement from the past through the present, modifying itself and proceeding further. That whole movement is thought and time, and that is limited. Its limited nature must create conflict, and is therefore one of the factors of the brain's deterioration. To inquire whether it is possible for the brain not to deteriorate at all, you must understand what the 'now' is.

What to you is the 'now'? The 'now' contains the past, the present and the future. The 'now' has no time. So, when you remain in the 'now', you understand the past with all its human experience of which you are. Your consciousness, with its content, is the past, the present and the future. Your consciousness is that, what you have been told and believe, programmed by politics, religion, education and so on, which means the past. And the past is there now. And the future is the outcome of that past – which is already here. The 'now' contains all time as past, present and future. Understand this in depth so that the 'now' contains the whole thing. All existence is now, so there is no movement away from the 'now'. There is no movement away from the fact to non-fact; any movement away from the fact to non-fact has ended. And so there is no conflict. I wonder if you understand all this. See the truth of it so that the brain, which has lived for thousands of years and is not your brain, not your thought, but the thought of the whole of humanity, is free of conflict.

The fact is now. And the fact contains all the past, the present and the future. But listen to that fact, for the fact to reveal its content – not you telling the fact what its content is. In the now, we are not only the past – all the memories and activities, the pain and anxiety, the loneliness, suffering and fears – you are all that now, and the future is what is now. So, the future and the past exist now because of what you are.

Aren't you the past? Your education, your being programmed as Swiss, British, German, Hindu, American, Russian and so on – that program is the past. The past is your accumulated memories. Those memories are stored in the brain, and so the past is now. The 'now' also contains the future, unless there is a fundamental mutation. That is, unless there is a complete mutation of the very cells of the brain, you are past memory and will continue in the future as memory. The future is therefore now, and the past is now, and that is how it will be unless there is fundamental, psychological change.

Memory is a movement of time – time as the future in the present. If you remain with the fact that you are *now*, and do not move away from it, you are the rest of all time. When you realise that, when the fact is revealed that you are that, and when you give your complete attention to it and do not escape from that, that memory is you. You are not different from that memory, so there is no division or conflict between you and that memory. The observer is the observed, the experiencer is the experience, and the analyser is the analysed. Then conflict ends. Conflict exists only when there is division, and when the brain is free of conflict, it ceases to deteriorate. But most of our brains have deteriorated or are deteriorating, and you have to discover why. What are the causes of deterioration? Essentially it is conflict. A brain that lives in fear – which we will discuss – such a brain must deteriorate. The brain that is seeking constant sensuality and sexuality must deteriorate. These are facts.

It is possible to find a way of living without the shadow of conflict. Then your brain is extraordinarily alive. Its activity then is whole because it is free. And the word *free* means also love. Love has no opposite. Is love desire? Is love the activity of thought? If it is, as with most of us, it is not love. If there is the activity of thought in relationship, there is no love.

CHAPTER 5

THE COMMON GROUND ON WHICH
ALL HUMAN BEINGS STAND.

We were talking about intelligence and security, and we came to the point that the past, present and future are contained in the 'now'. That is, all time is now. And in the 'now' there is no time at all.

We ought to consider the future of humanity. Through various series of events, vast experience and collective memory – the whole process of time from the infinite past to the present – we have arrived at the current stage of human evolution. And what is our future? Not only the future of each one of us – and I question whether each one of us is separate from humanity as a whole – but what lies ahead of us all? Do we proceed more or less along the same path taken for the last million years, slowly developing, slowly accumulating vast memories?

Considering what evolution has brought us to now, what are the successive events and experiences that lie ahead of us? We have evolved, and are almost primitive psychologically – angry, violent, having countless illusions, dogmas, beliefs, faiths of various religions and various movements, societies and cultures – all that is inherited by us. That is what we are, unquestionably. Nobody can argue or theoretically dispute that we are the result of vast, successive experiences, incidents and so on. That is our consciousness; we are that. And from the beginning of time, we have not changed very much – biologically we have reached a certain point. When we look at ourselves and the society we have created, the divisions we have brought about religiously, nationally, tribally and all the rest of it, I wonder what the future of human beings will be.

This is a very serious question which we ought to consider and investigate together. You and I are walking together along the same road, at the same pace, with the same intention, with the same commitment to finding out the future of humanity. Not only the future of our grandchildren, and their grandchildren and so on, but the whole of humanity – not our own particular future.

Our consciousness, which is what we are – our reactions, our psychological and physical responses, all the beliefs of various cultures and peoples, all the faiths, the dogmas, the environmental conditioning, our fears, anxieties, loneliness, depression, sorrows and the constant pain of conflict – is the common ground on which all human beings stand. That is a fact. When you suffer, when you are lonely, depressed, anxious, in conflict with your friend, wife or husband, this is the lot of humans worldwide. Whether you live in Asia, America or Europe, every one of us goes through this. Another may express it differently, may put it in words unfamiliar to you, but the feeling, the pain, anxiety, sorrow, uncertainty, insecurity, faith in something illusory that has no reality, the vast network of superstition, is the common lot of all human beings. This is our consciousness.

Your consciousness is not therefore something private, personal, exclusive to yourself. It is shared by all human beings. Whether you go to the most deprived parts of Africa or the most sophisticated part of New York or Tokyo, everyone shares this consciousness. Having a belief in something or other is not exclusive to you; belief is shared by everybody. Another may believe in one thing and you may believe in something else, but belief is common to all of us. Pain, tears, laughter, anxiety, humour, a sense of desperate loneliness, are shared by every human being on this beautiful earth. These states are not yours, and this consciousness is the self, the person, the 'me', the ego.

This ego is the common ego of humanity. This is a very difficult truth for most people to see and accept because we are all conditioned to believe that we are separate human beings with separate souls – a belief that religions have encouraged. When we think, we think as though we are separate from everyone else who thinks. But as we have said, thinking is common to all of us, whether the highly educated, sophisticated philosopher or the most uneducated person. Thinking is common to all of us and is not therefore your individual, private thinking. It is very difficult for people to accept who have been brought up from childhood to think that they are separate from others. That is a marvellous illusion, cultivated sedulously through literature, talent, religion, worship of your nation and all the rest of it. And this common consciousness is the collective self – not your self, the self which everybody clings to.

What is the future of humanity? What is going to happen to our brain when computers and robots take over, and when big industry invents ultra-intelligent machines? What is the future of human beings if we don't change inwardly? They are going to change you from the outside – it is inevitable, it is on the cards. We laypeople know little about what they are doing, and perhaps we don't want to know. So, what is going to happen to our brain? The human brain, not the mechanical brain invented and controlled by top computer experts, biochemists and genetic engineers acting from the outside. We are not painting a dark picture; it is happening. So, what is the future of man? Your theories, your gurus, your doctrines, your Churches, will have no place at all because the computer brain is much more active and much clearer. It will answer a question in a millionth of a second. Take all this in, without being frightened or depressed by it, but seeing the actual fact of what is going on.

Our brain is now conditioned by experience, by successive incidents that bring about fear and pleasure, aches and anxieties, the pain of sorrow and death. We are also conditioned linguistically and climatically. This is our conditioning and we assume that in the course of evolution we will gradually change inwardly – which means continue almost indefinitely as we are. Any alternative, a sudden jump, is regarded as psychologically impossible. Can we, even a few of us, change, bring about a mutation in the very cells of the brain? Does it take time? Does it take a series of incidents, successive memories, to bring about a mutation in the conditioning?

Please bear in mind that in investigating condition-ing, we are not investigating personal conditioning but the general conditioning of the human brain. We are not talking about an individual transformation or mutation that will make you more enlightened or happier – nonsense like that. We are talking about the human brain because you, as a human being, represent all humanity. You are all humanity because you suffer and all others suffer. You are humanity, not just one isolated, individual, secretive person concerned with your own little self.

Now, if we don't radically bring about a psycho-logical revolution in the sense of a mutation, we will find that our brains will wither because the computer and robot, and other devices being invented, will make our brains inactive. At present you have to think, investigate and work, meaning your brain has to be active. But when the computer and robot take things over, what is going to happen to your brain? It is going to wither and indulge in endless entertainment. Or will you investigate whether, as a human being who is the rest of humanity, there is a radical mutation by which you affect the whole of human consciousness?

I do not know if you have noticed how when something is invented in one country, the rest of the world soon picks it up too. If one or two, a dozen or a hundred, bring about fundamental freedom from conditioning, they will affect the whole of human consciousness. This is so. Hitler, Napoleon and religious leaders have affected humanity, the whole of human consciousness.

So, after stating all this, can we bring about — not through a gradual process of evolution, that is out! — a mutation in our whole being, in our whole behaviour, in our way of looking at life?

This means we have to investigate together the content of our consciousness — of which you are because its content makes up consciousness. Without its content, consciousness as we know it doesn't exist. If I am a Hindu, with all the business of superstitions, gods, rituals, that circus, like the Christians with their faith, belief and habits, then can all that be radically, totally changed?

Please, this is very serious. This is not something to play with. See the danger of what, from the outside, they are going to do to our brains, and also see actually what our brains are: conditioned nationally, linguistically, by fear, pleasure, sorrow and by faith; I believe, I don't believe, my prejudice is better than your prejudice and so on. That is what we are. And one of the contents of our consciousness is fear, which is shared by all human beings.

What is fear? How does it arise? Please, you are sharing this, we are thinking together; I am not the explorer, with you just listening and playing with words. You are afraid; that is a fact. Afraid to die, afraid to lose, afraid not to become something, afraid of your wife or husband, or somebody or other, afraid of nature. Fear. And can that fear, which has conditioned our brain, end completely? Not through time, not gradually through evolution.

Fear does terrible things. It makes you lie, it makes you kill, it makes you violent, it makes you curl up in yourself. All of us know what fear is. Is one of the causes of fear wanting to become something psychologically? That is, I am this and I must be that. 'That' is a projection through comparison. I compare myself with you and I want to be like you. Or I don't want to be like you but would like to be like somebody else — to become. Comparing is to become.

Can we now end all comparison? Of course, you have to compare two cars. If you have the money you buy the better one. When you are comparing one house with another, and so on, it is necessary to get the best materials, the better of the houses, if you have the money. But we are talking about psychological comparison, seeing the consequences of comparison, which is to become. This is one of the causes of fear. And seeing the truth of it, end instantly all comparison – are you doing it? Even a few of you, so that your brain is free of this burden, which means unconditioning the brain cells themselves. Those cells have been accustomed, trained, educated to compare: one day you will sit next to God – you know all that stuff – or you compare what you are with what you should be. To end comparison so the sense of ideals and the future end completely. And that means one of the causes of fear ends instantly.

There are other multiple causes of fear – fear of public opinion, fear of what your friends might say about you – you know, a thousand fears – fear of the dark, fear of your wife or husband, fear of your guru because you want to be like him. You are always trying to become something, but what is it that is becoming? An idea, a memory, a thought? Hence it is an empty becoming; there is nothing in it and yet we cling to that. Is time another cause of fear? Fear of the future or fear of the past, fear of having done something – biological fears and psychological fears are based on the past, which is time. And there is fear of the future as death. So time and thought are the roots of fear.

Do we see the fact that comparison, thought and time are the basic factors of fear? If you then say, 'How am I to stop thinking?' that is a wrong question. When you see a dangerous snake in front of you, you act; you don't ask, 'What am I to do? Please tell me how to run from it.' When there is danger, there is an instant response. And time and thought in relation to fear is a tremendous danger. But do you actually see the danger itself, or the *idea* of danger? The idea is stronger than the fact and so we play with it. The idea of a snake is different from the actual snake. Like a precipice: you can imagine you are standing on the edge of a precipice and play around with falling, but when you have a real, deep chasm at your feet, you respond instantly. If you are aware of the nature and danger of fear, how it corrupts the mind . . . *the brain* – the mind is different – sorry for using the word *mind*; I will keep the mind away from the brain – do you see the danger to the brain and therefore act?

Also, you have to consider the whole pursuit of pleasure – the becoming, the achieving, being attached to something, possessing something – sexual pleasure and the various forms of pleasure. When you are attached, when you are tied to something, corruption begins. When I am tied to my wife or husband, or to an ideal or a series of logical, deductive conclusions, and I hold onto that, corruption is inevitable. When I hold onto or am attached to my wife or girlfriend because I get comfort, sex and all the rest of it, in that attachment, that tie, is the seed of corruption. See the truth that wherever there is any kind of attachment to anything – to your furniture, a person, an ideal, a system; any attachment or tie to anything – you already have the flowering of corruption. And pleasure is corruption if you are pursuing it. If pleasure happens, all right, but if you pursue it, as most human beings do, and are attached to pleasure, then the whole corruptive process takes place, which brings about deterioration of the brain. Corruption is deterioration.

We ought also to talk over together a much more complex problem, that of suffering. Human beings, wherever they live, have suffered enormously. Go to poor countries where they do not have enough to eat, one meal a day – they suffer infinitely. And with the wars of many centuries, how many people have been killed, how many tears shed! There is the sorrow of not achieving, the sorrow of ignorance – not of books or professorial knowledge; we are talking of ignorance of the truth, of reality, of what is going on inwardly. There is the sorrow of losing somebody you think you love, the sorrow of disease, the sorrow of a thousand things. Humankind all over the world has borne this sorrow and we are still going on with it. What is wrong with us? We know the wars, the maimed victims, those terrible tanks and pilots dropping a bomb from 30,000 feet, not seeing the devastation it makes and saying at the end of it, 'God was with me the day I dropped the atom bomb on Hiroshima.'

Is it possible to end sorrow? Which is to face it and end it – not take time to analyse the causes of sorrow, seeking comfort. There is always a comforter: a priest, a psychoanalyst, a friend, a guru, someone to cry with you or hold your hand. That doesn't end sorrow. It is like having a deep wound; you may cover it up or escape from it but it is always there, deep down in the dark recesses of your brain. While there is suffering there is no love, and without love and compassion, there is no intelligence.

If we continue our daily life as we are living now, year after year until we die, as billions of people are doing, we are not contributing anything new to the collective consciousness of humanity. That will only happen if you and a few of us basically, fundamentally, bring about a mutation in the conditioning of the brain, in the very cells themselves. And that is possible only when we are aware of our conditioning and meet it head-on: the sorrow, the fear, the faiths and the dogmas, the stupid rituals, the pleasures, of which we are. If there is no such mutation we will be contributing to the ugliness of humanity. There is only one choice for us really, only one direction: either mutate or give ourselves up to the world of entertainment — football, literature, art, cinema — the vast entertainment industry that is gradually taking us over. And that industry includes the rituals of religious people — which are a form of entertainment. People don't change by going week after week to Mass, or to the Indian rituals.

There is a temple in India near the school we visit. It is one of the most famous in India. They take vows to the image inside and pour in thousands of dollars a day. It has become a tremendous business affair — just as all religion has.

When you actually see all this, spread out in front of you like a clear map: the computer and robot, biochemistry, genetic engineering and brain research, and the vast range of entertainment — unless you are extraordinarily aware you are going to be caught in it all. Probably you are already. But when there is a change, a radical mutation in the conditioning, which means freedom from all conditioning, that freedom is love. That freedom is compassion, a compassion that is not attached to any religion. It is not because I love Jesus or Krishna or somebody that I am compassionate. Compassion is only born out of total freedom.

CHAPTER 6

RELIGION AND MEDITATION. SEEING WHEN
THOUGHT IS A SOURCE OF CONFLICT. THE ENDING
OF PSYCHOLOGICAL MEASUREMENT.

We can only inquire into what religion is when we have established order in our lives. Now we live in disorder: confused, uncertain, driven by various desires, and we generally muddle along in disorder. That disorder may have its own order – trains and aircraft leave more or less on time, and telephones connect directly with the other side of the world. There is some order in the world's disorder, but in our lives there can only be total order when there is freedom from fear, from all the hurts received since childhood, together with an understanding of the meaning and pursuit of pleasure, of becoming and of the ending of sorrow. Only then, when there is freedom and order, can you really ask: What is religion?

If we ask this while living a disorderly, scatter-brained life, we will invent, as we have done, religious orthodoxies and religions like Christianity and Islam based on books. In India, they have thousands of gods. That is much more fun than having one. Then you can play with them all! Today you choose one that pleases you, next week another and so on – you can go through the whole lot for years, choosing your own gods. And what we call religion – established, orthodox, organised, faith-based – has nothing to do with our daily life. They create a make-believe world, a romantic, sentimental, imaginative, superficially comforting world. So out of chaotic disorder, we bring about religions that are very comforting but have no validity, no fundamental meaning in daily life. You engage in it as you would in some kind of entertainment and sensation, with the constant repetition of rituals, the use of incense – you know all that.

I generally put religion and meditation at the end of the talks, because over the five we have already had, we have covered the structure and business of life, and perhaps some of us are deeply free of fear and no longer carry any psychological wounds. Perhaps some of us have understood the futility of pursuing pleasure, and perhaps some have grasped the significance of suffering and its ending, and so have the extraordinary qualities of love and compassion. When there is order in our life not induced by thought, then only can we ask what religion is. Thought can never bring about order; only perception of fact can and nothing else, which needs a clear, unprejudiced, unbiased brain. If you are afraid, in order to escape from it you can invent anything you like, something very comforting and satisfying – which is what most of us do. Yet that invention, that imaginative structure of something higher, is born out of fear and is therefore nothing whatsoever to do with religion or with a religious brain.

The etymological meaning of the word *religion* has not been clearly established. If you look it up in a dictionary, they haven't been able to trace the early beginnings of the word. They have given various meanings at different times, but it really means gathering all your energy. I am saying that, not the dictionary.

So, we will go into the nature of religion, and in doing so we will discover what meditation is. Not as something outside our daily life – that again becomes extraordinarily superficial. Or you may think that having the right kind of meditation will affect your daily life. Whereas if you understand its significance, meditation is extraordinarily important, not as a practice and all the silly nonsense that goes on, but its deep significance.

Is this clear so far, so that we can proceed together? Not that I go on and you just sleepily follow me, but we are sharing responsibility for finding out what religion is, what place it has in daily life, and in so doing discovering for ourselves the depth and beauty of meditation – discovering it for ourselves, not being told about it by the various gurus bringing their latest systems of meditation for which you pay, which seems so absurdly commercial.

Before we go into religion and meditation, we ought to understand what it means to listen. Do we, each one of us, listen, hear, what we say to each other? You are wanting to tell me something and I want to tell you something, so there is a battle going on. You want to say something to another and have not the time or inclination or intention to listen, so you never listen to the other person. There is this constant deafness, no sense of space, meaning we don't listen to each other.

Hearing is not only with the ear but also listening to the meaning, significance and sound of the word. Its sound is very important. When there is sound, there is space. The art of listening, if I may point out most respectfully, is not only hearing but also listening to the sound of the word. To listen to that sound, there must be space. But if you listen and translate what is said into your own prejudices, your own pleasing or displeasing scheme of things, then you are not listening at all. So, can we attempt to listen not only to what I am saying but also to our own reaction to what is said, and in so doing, not correct that reaction in order to conform to what is said?

I am saying something you are listening to, and you are also listening to your reaction to it while giving space to the sound of your own reaction. This needs tremendous attention, not going off into a kind of trance and saying, 'It was very nice this morning, a marvellous talk. I am glad I was there, he told me a lot of things I hadn't thought about.' Whereas if you really listen, in that listening is a miracle. The miracle is that you are completely with the fact of what is being said, listening to that and listening also to your own response. It is a simultaneous process. You listen to what is being said and to your reaction to it, which is instantaneous, and listen to the whole sound of it, which means having space. Then you are giving your whole attention to listening. This is an art not learnt by going to college to get a degree in listening, but by listening to everything: to the river flowing by, to the birds, to the aircraft, to your wife or husband – which is far more difficult, because you have got used to each other and you almost know what they are going to say. And they know very well what you are going to say! Then you have shut your hearing off altogether.

Here we are talking of something entirely different: the art of listening, learning about it now. That is, to listen, to be aware of your own responses and allow space. Listening is a total process, not a separate one, but a unitary movement. This is an art that demands your highest attention. When you so attend, there is no listener, only the fact, the reality or falseness of the fact. I hope we are doing this now because we are going into something very complex. Of course, if you want to go off into a romantic trance, that is all right, but if you really want to probe into the nature of a brain that is religious and meditative, you have to listen very, very attentively to everything. There is no difference between the noise of the aircraft, the noise I am making and the noise you are making. It is like a tremendous river moving.

We are investigating what religion is. Is it a structure of thought, or is it beyond thought? As we have said and understood, thought is always based on experience, knowledge and memory, and is very limited. That is clear. Anything projected, put together by thought, is also always limited. The various religions of the world have been put together by thought. You may say they are a divine revelation, straight from the horse's mouth, and to convey that, it is expressed in thought and put down on paper. But whether that paper is two thousand or five thousand years old, it is still the activity of thought. All the rigmarole, the words and the rituals — the whole structure of this movement is based on thought. You can sanctify what thought has created and worship it, calling it religious, which only shows how the brain is caught in a process of illusion.

If we are clear on that point, let us now try to find out what religion is that is not put together by limited thought. When you accept your guru and do all the things they say, it is very, very limited. They might talk about illumination and leading you to truth, but it is still the activity of thought. You cannot belong to any guru, follow any system or method, because they are all the product of thought. To examine that which is beyond thought . . . not thought examining it; there lies the difficulty.

I see that the activity of thought is limited, entirely so, in any direction, whether in computer technology or psychologically. Thought, with all its activity, is limited, and therefore there must be conflict. That is understood. And that being understood, what is the instrument that can probe into something that is not the activity of thought? Is it possible? Careful please, we are working together; put your whole brain into this.

Thought can investigate its own activity, its own limitation, its own process of putting things together, destroying that and creating something else – thought in its own confusion can bring about a certain order, but that order too is limited. It is not supreme order that relates to the whole business of existence.

So, *probe* and *investigate* are perhaps the wrong words to use because you cannot investigate something that is beyond thought. You can write books about it, and get a big kick out of that, playing that kind of game everlastingly. Theologians and overexcited people do that sort of stuff. But find out whether it is possible to observe without any movement of thought. Just to observe; observe a tree, listen to the river, which is part of observing, without any interference from the words *tree, river* – to observe without any movement of past remembrance entering into the observing, which requires complete freedom from the past as the observer. Just to observe. Are we understanding each other? Let's go into it a little more.

When you look at your wife or husband, your friend or a passing train, the wife or husband, the friend or the train have a particular name. This name is associated with memory, which is time. Memory can take place only during the interval between the incident and the remembrance, which is time. So, can you listen and observe without the whole movement of thought, which is time? Can you do it? Don't say it is not possible or is possible. You have to observe, you have to see actually how you look at a tree or at a cloud lit by the morning sun, full of depth, beauty, light and tremendous activity, look without the words *tree* or *cloud*. That is fairly easy because it has nothing to do with you. You can look at the tree, cloud or river without the word. The word *river* is not that river; it stands for all the rivers in the world. If you associate the word *river* with one particular river, you can never then understand the whole movement of rivers.

Can you observe without the word? Which means to observe without all the remembrances and associations the word implies. Can you look at your wife or girlfriend, husband or boyfriend, without the word *wife* or *girlfriend*, *husband* or *boyfriend* – without all the remembrances the word contains, so that you look at her or him, or at the river, as though for the first time?

When you wake up in the morning and look out of your window, it is an astonishing sight when you look as though you were just born. Which means to observe without any bias, without any conclusion or prejudice. Will you do that as we are talking? And you cannot do this if you are only half-awake. Again, the window view demands not too much attention and therefore you do it easily, but if I look at my wife or husband with all the images, incidents, memories and hurts, I never look at them. I am always looking from the viewpoint of these images and memories – I look at them through all that. Can you look as though for the first time, without the images and memories?

We are going to observe the nature of a religious brain, a brain that is not contaminated by thought. This demands your utmost attention, which means you are totally, completely free from any commitment – to your guru, to your Church, to your ideas, to your past tradition, completely free of that in order to observe. When you so observe, what has taken place in the very nature of the brain?

Please first understand the question before we go further. I have always looked at the tree, at the river, at the sky, at the beauty of a cloud, my wife or husband, my children, with a remembrance, with an image. That is my conditioning. And you come along and tell me: look without the word, without the image, without all the past remembrances. And I say, 'I can't do it.' The first, immediate response is, 'I can't do it.' This means you are not actually listening to what the man is saying; your response is instantaneous. Now, the point is to be aware, to be attentive to saying, 'I can't do it,' which is a form of resistance. So pay attention to the 'I can't do it' and also listen to what the other man is saying: that to observe there must be complete freedom from the word, the content of the word. Listen to both.

There is the movement of resistance and the listening, or wanting to listen. And you cannot listen if you are resisting. So be aware, don't move from that, don't say, 'I must understand' – just watch it so that you bring about total attention.

I hope you are sitting comfortably and paying attention to what is being said so that you can observe, an observation without the movement of thought. Are you doing it? Or it is just another theory, another case of wanting to do something like meditation and saying, 'Tell me how to do it, what is the method, what is the system?' That is all rather childish. This observation is pure observation without the movement of the self. The word is the self. The word, the remembrances, the accumulated hurts, fears, anxieties, pains, sorrows, and all the travail of human existence are the self, which is your consciousness. And when you observe, all this is gone. All this doesn't enter into it; there is no 'me' observing. Then in that observation in daily life, there is perfect order, there is no contradiction. Contradiction is disorder. I hope this is clear and we are not going off into a trance.

Let's proceed. What is meditation? Not how to meditate. When you ask 'how' that implies somebody telling you what to do. If you don't ask how, but ask what meditation is, you then have to exert your own capacity, your own experience, however limited – you have to think. Otherwise you may say, 'Tell me what meditation is,' so you can go off into some kind of silly dream. The word *meditation* means to ponder, to think over, to be concerned with, and also to be dedicated – not *to* something but the spirit of dedication. And the root of *meditation* also means to measure, in Sanskrit, Latin and Greek. Now, what is the meaning of the word *measure*? We live by measure. Measure is time, isn't it? I measure myself, what I am now and what I should be. That is a measurement.

What matters is to find out for yourself and to stand by that and not depend on anybody. To do that, you must understand very carefully the meaning of the word *measure*. What does it imply? From the ancient Greeks to our times, measurement has been essential in engineering. Our technology is based on measurement. You cannot possibly put together a bridge without measurement, or construct a marvellous hundred-storey building without measurement. And we are also measuring inwardly: I have been, I will be; I have been this, I must be that – which is not only measurement but comparison. Measurement is comparison. You are tall and I am short, I am fair and you are brown – measurement. Please understand the meaning of measurement, and the words *better* and *more* – understand those two words and never use *better* and *more* inwardly. Is this clear? Have you understood the meaning of the word *measure?* Let us consider it together. That means you and I are willing to let go of our prejudices and think it over together, to see the depth of the word *measure*. We have touched on it briefly. I don't want to get into details, but see the meaning of that.

So, when the brain is free of measurement, do you see what has happened? The very brain cells which have been used to measuring, which are conditioned to measure, have suddenly awakened to the truth, the fact that measurement is psychologically destructive, and have therefore undergone a mutation.

My brain has been used to going in a certain direction – let us say used to going northeast – and I think that is the only way to whatever there is at the end of it. Naturally, what is at the end of it is what I invent. Then you come along and tell me that the direction of northeast will lead me nowhere. I resist, I say, 'No, you are wrong. All tradition, all the great writers, all the great saints say you are wrong.' This means I really haven't investigated, but am quoting somebody else. Which means I am resisting. Then you say to me, 'Don't resist; listen to what I am saying, and also listen to what you are thinking, what your reaction is. Listen to both.' And to listen to both you must give attention, which means space.

Find out, not at moments of some peculiar meditation but in daily life, whether you can live without measurement. Do you understand what that implies? Never to use the words *better* or *more*: 'I am more than I was, I am better than I was yesterday.' Silly nonsense! 'I am less angry, I have disciplined myself a little more today.' This is what we are all doing in various ways. But meditation is to live a life without any sense of measurement. And to think together, to ponder together, to be concerned together.

Meditation implies a sense of deep understanding of measurement. That very understanding and perception, or insight into that, is the action that ends psychological measurement.

Don't we measure? If we are honest with ourselves, aren't we always measuring? Can you live a daily life without psychological measurement, without comparison? This means the brain cells, which have been accustomed all their life to measuring, suddenly end it, and there is a mutation in the cells. Do at least see the logical, intellectual fact of this.

Your brain is mechanical, responding to various programs, propaganda and so on; your brain has become stuck in a routine, going to the office from nine to five, and so on. Your brain cells have been conditioned. And to break that conditioning instantly, not by evolution through time, is to listen to something totally new. That is, to have no measurement psychologically. When you see that fact without any resistance, that very perception brings about a radical change in the very structure of the cells.

What else is meditation? We have understood the meaning of the word: to be concerned, to ponder, think over, look together, and we have also understood the meaning of the word *measure* – never to say, 'I am dull, you are clever,' and so on. And when you do grasp that, then you are what you are, and from there you can move. If I am imitating you because you are clever, I am dull in comparison. I am imitating, which is not cleverness itself. If I don't compare at all with you who are clever, I don't then call myself dull – I am what I am. From there I can begin. But if I am copying you, I have nowhere to start, I am just pursuing you.

What is next in meditation? We have understood the nature of attention, of total listening. To listen there must be space and there must be sound in that space.

Is there something sacred, holy? We are not saying there is or there isn't. Is there something never touched by thought? Not that 'I' have reached something beyond thought, but is there something that is beyond thought? Which is not matter because thought is a material process. Anything that is put together by thought is limited, and therefore isn't complete, isn't the whole. Is there something that is completely out of the world of thought?

We are inquiring together, giving our attention, listening – which means what? All the activity of thought has ended, except in the physical world where I have to do certain things, go from here to there, write a letter, drive a car, get food, cook, wash dishes – there I have to use limited, routine thought. But inwardly, psychologically, there can be no further activity unless thought has come completely to an end. To observe anything beyond thought, thought must come to an end. But it is not ending thought through a method, concentration or control.

The necessity to find out if there is something more than thought, that very necessity creates the energy which then ends thought. The importance of ending thought in order to observe further, that very importance brings about the ending of thought. It is as simple as that. Don't complicate it. This is important because thought, which is limited, has its own space, its own order. When the activity of limited thought ceases, then there is space, not only in the brain but space. Not the space that the self creates around itself, but limitless space. When thought discovers for itself its limitation, and sees that its limitation is creating havoc in the world, that very observation brings thought to an end, because you want to discover something new.

An engineer who knows all about the internal combustion engine, who has worked with it for years and says, 'I want to discover something,' has to put all that aside to see something new. If he carries that with him all the time, he cannot see anything new. That is how the jet engine was discovered. The man who discovered it understood internal combustion completely and said there must be something new. He was watching, waiting, listening, and came upon something new. Similarly, you see that thought is limited, and whatever it does will always be limited. Because by its very nature it is conditioned and therefore limited, the machinery of thought cannot go beyond itself. So thought says, 'If I have the urge to go further, that machinery must come to a stop.' Then the ending of thought begins. Then there is space and silence.

Meditation is the understanding of the meaning of measurement, and the ending of psychological measurement which is becoming – the ending of that and seeing that thought is everlastingly limited. It may think of the limitless but that is born of limitation. Measurement comes to an end, and the brain that has been chattering along, muddled, limited, has suddenly become silent without any compulsion or discipline because it sees the fact and truth of its limitation. That fact and truth, as we pointed out, are beyond time. And so thought comes to an end.

Then there is a sense of absolute silence in the brain. All the movement of thought has ended. It has ended but can be brought into activity when necessary in the physical world. But now it is quiet, silent. Where there is silence there must be space, immense space, because there is no self from which . . . Do you get it? The self has its own limited space. When you are thinking about yourself, it creates its own little space. But when the self is not, which means that the activity of thought has ceased, there is vast silence in the brain because it is now free from all its conditioning. And only where there is space and silence can there be something new, untouched by time and thought. That may be the most holy, the most sacred. May be. You cannot give it a name. It is perhaps the unnameable. And when there is that, there is intelligence, compassion and love. Life is no longer fragmented; it is a whole, unitary, moving, living process.

Everything from the very beginning of these talks until now is part of meditation because we have gone into human nature and the bringing about of a radical mutation. And that nobody can do except you yourself.

PART TWO

Questions and Answers

INTRODUCTION

How do you approach a problem? Life has many problems: economic, social, religious, technological, personal — how do you approach them? The word *approach* means to draw near, come close to. And from Latin and Greek, the root meaning of the word also means something thrown at you, a challenge. Now, how do you receive that challenge? If you approach a problem in the trance of tradition — that's a good phrase! — then you will never solve it. On the contrary, the problem remains and you inject more problems into it — which is what is happening in politics. Or if you approach a problem having already drawn a conclusion, then obviously one doesn't meet its challenge. The same failure occurs if you approach it with an ideological belief. Whether the problem is technological, social, religious or personal, unless you approach it without any motive, the solution will have very little significance. What matters therefore is how you approach it because the approach is going to dictate the outcome.

We are not telling you what to do. I am not your guru to follow. I am not important, but what I say is important, as it is for you to find out whether it is false or true. You must have a great capacity to be sceptical, to doubt, to question, so that your mind is sharp and clear.

We are going to answer some of the questions put. They involve problems and we, you and I, are going to approach them without any personal motive, without the deadening weight of tradition, bias or prejudice. Then your brain is free to look at the problem. When that is clear, let's examine these questions together. They are not problems for myself, but as they are for the questioners, and for most people, we will act together. So there is no leader and the led. There is no guru sitting on a platform. Fortunately, I have no beard, strange robes or any of that kind of nonsense! So let us together go into the questions without any bias, tradition or prejudice.

CHAPTER 7

YOU HAVE SAID TO US 'YOU ARE THE WORLD AND
YOU ARE TOTALLY RESPONSIBLE FOR THE WHOLE OF
MANKIND.' HOW CAN THIS IDEA BE JUSTIFIED ON A
RATIONAL, OBJECTIVE, SANE BASIS?

I am not sure it can be justified on a rational, sane,
objective basis. We will examine it first before we say
it can.

As we have said, the earth on which we live is our
earth, it is not the British earth or the French, German, Russian, Indian or Chinese earth, it is our earth
on which we are all living. That is a fact. But thought
has divided it racially, geographically, culturally and
economically. This division is causing havoc in the
world. That cannot be denied; it is rational, objective,
sane. It is our earth on which we are all living, though
politically and economically we have divided it for
security and for various patriotic, illusory reasons,
which eventually bring about war.

We have also said that human consciousness is similar. Please go into this with me, you may disagree, you may say it is all nonsense, but please listen and see whether this is rational, objective and sane. All human consciousness is similar. We all, on whatever part of the earth we live, go through a great deal of suffering, pain, anxiety, uncertainty and fear. And occasionally, perhaps often, we have pleasure. This is the common ground on which all human beings stand. That is an irrefutable fact. We may try to dodge it, saying, 'No, I am an individual,' and so on, but when you look at it objectively, impersonally, not as British, French and so on, you will find that the consciousness of all human beings is similar, psychologically speaking.

This is the common ground on which all humanity stands. And we are responsible for whatever happens in the field of this consciousness. That is, if I am violent, I am adding violence to this consciousness common to all of us. If I am not violent, not adding to it, I am bringing about a totally new factor in that consciousness. I am profoundly responsible either for contributing to that violence, that confusion, that terrible division, or I recognise deeply in my heart, my blood, in the depth of my being that I am as the rest of the world, I am humankind, I am the world, the world is not separate from me. Then I become totally responsible, which is rational, objective, sane. The other response is insanity, to call yourself a Hindu, a Buddhist, a Christian – they are just labels.

When you have that feeling, that reality, see the truth of it, that every human being living on this earth is responsible not only for themselves but responsible for everything that is happening, how will you translate this into daily life? If you have that feeling as an intellectual conclusion, as an ideal, then it has no reality, but if you see you are standing on ground common to all of us, and you feel totally responsible, then what is your action towards society, towards the world you are living in? The world as it is now is full of violence. Only very few people escape from it because they are carefully guarded, protected and all the rest of it.

So, suppose I realise that I am totally responsible. What then do I do? Competition between nations, the most powerful and the less powerful, is destroying the world – with the less powerful trying to become more powerful. Shall I, realising that I am the rest of humanity and am totally responsible, be competitive? Please answer these questions. When I feel responsible, I naturally cease to be competitive. Also, the religious world, as well as the economic and social world, is based on the hierarchical principle. Will I also adopt this concept of hierarchy? Obviously not, because that again means there is one who says, 'I know,' with the other saying, 'I do not know.' The one who says 'I know' takes a superior position, economically, socially, religiously, and has status. If that is what you want, go after it, but you will contribute to the confusion in the world.

There are actual, objective, sane actions when you perceive, when you realise in your heart of hearts, in the depth of your being, that you are the rest of mankind and that we are all standing on the same ground.

CHAPTER 8

WHAT IS PSYCHOLOGICAL TIME, AND WHY IS IT A SOURCE OF CONFLICT?

Let us consider together what time is. Time by the watch, time by the sun setting and rising, time as yesterday, today and tomorrow – that tomorrow may be a hundred years ahead, and yesterday may be a hundred years ago, and the time today is that we are sitting here. There is time, physically, in the acquisition of knowledge, in so-called evolution. Time is necessary to learn a language or to become a physicist. Time is necessary to drive a car. Time is necessary, that is obvious. Now, is it that we carry this idea of time – which we have established naturally, logically, because I need time to learn a technique – into the psychological realm? Or does psychological time exist in itself? Does time as a process of psychological evolution exist in itself?

Please, let us be quite clear on this: is there psychological time in itself, intrinsically? Or have we carried over the time factor necessary to learn a skill into the psychological area? That is, does time exist psychologically *per se,* or have we introduced time because of our conditioning in the technical area and therefore react in the same manner in the psychological area? Is time inherent in the psychological realm, or has thought brought the time factor into it? Has thought introduced into the psychological realm the whole idea of time, or is time in the very nature of the psyche?

Thought, which is part of the psyche, has introduced time into the psychological realm: I am this, I will be that; I am angry, I will get over it; I am not successful but I will be. All of that movement is time – the distance covered from what I am to what I shall be, the space between me as I am and me as I will be. Time is the space to be covered to achieve that; the whole process of that is time. I do not know myself so I must learn about myself, educate myself. The same thing is operating in the case of a skill. So, time is a factor of thought, and thought is the response of experience, knowledge and memory stored in the brain. That memory responds in thought. Again, this is an obvious fact. And we have accumulated a great deal of knowledge psychologically which is stored in the brain as memory and thought.

So, this whole process of accumulating knowledge about yourself, gradually building information about yourself, implies time. There is psychological time, and there is time by the day and by the watch – psychological time and chronological time. Now, is this element of time inherent in the psyche, in being and becoming? I am putting this in different ways. Please don't jump to the conclusion that there is in us a timeless state. I am not saying that at all. That is the old tradition. We are not saying that, we are just asking.

Is the 'me' free of time? Obviously not. The 'me' – my family, my nation, my character, my capacity, my loneliness, my despair – my whole travail in being is 'me', the 'me' that is going to die, the 'me' that lives, going to the office, laboratory, factory, whatever you are doing. All that is the activity of thought, including the 'me'. The 'me' is my form, my name, the image I have about myself, the things I have done, the things I want to do, etc. All that is 'me', which is my consciousness. The content of that consciousness is put there by thought, which is time.

There is psychological time, which is the movement of thought, fear, pleasure, pain, suffering, joy and so-called love. All that is the movement of thought, thought being memory, space, time, achievement. Now, we are saying that psychological time is the factor of conflict and sorrow.

As we have been pointing out, thought is the root of fear, and thought is the root of pleasure. I have had pleasure yesterday. There is remembrance and the desire to continue it tomorrow. That is the movement of thought. And sorrow, as we said, is the essence of isolation. Sorrow is the outcome of self-centred egotistic activity. Thought is responsible for this, and thought is psychological time itself. Is it possible to be free of psychological time? Because that divides, and where there is division there must be conflict. Wherever there is division there must be conflict. That is a law. It is not my law; it is there.

So thought, time and space, psychologically, are the source of conflict and sorrow. After examining it, is it possible for thought to realise its own place, which is in the area of technique, and with no place psychologically? Please don't reject this, just look at it.

Psychological time exists when I have an image of myself. You tread on that image, causing a wound that hurts. That is an element of time. If I have no image of myself, it is finished. Now, is that possible living in this world, married, and all the rest of it? That is to have no tomorrow. It is not like Dante talking about those who enter Inferno abandoning hope – it is not that at all. Why do we have hope? I am not saying you shouldn't or should, but why do we have hope? See what happens. I hope to be a great person or whatever it is – it is my hope. And I am working for that. I may fail. We generally do. Then I get bitter, angry, violent, cynical. And by adding violence, cynicism and bitterness to the confusion of the total human consciousness, I am perpetuating that confusion. But if I have an insight into this, the image dissolves entirely.

CHAPTER 9

IF TWO PEOPLE HAVE A RELATIONSHIP OF CONFLICT
AND PAIN, CAN THEY RESOLVE IT OR MUST THE
RELATIONSHIP END? AND TO HAVE A GOOD
RELATIONSHIP, ISN'T IT NECESSARY FOR
BOTH TO CHANGE?

I hope the question is clear. What is the cause of pain and conflict, and of all the problems that arise in relationship? What is the root of it? Please, in answering this, we are thinking together. It is a question that concerns human beings whether in the East or West.

Apparently, two people cannot live together without conflict and pain, without a sense of inequality or a feeling they are not profoundly related to each other. Why? There may be multiple causes for this lack of harmony: sex, temperament, opposed feelings, beliefs, ambition. But what is the real source, at depth, that brings about conflict in each of us? That is the important question to ask.

I ask myself why, if I am married or have a partner, do we have this basic conflict between us? I can give superficial answers, but I want to find out what the deep root, the deep source of this conflict is between people. I have put this question and I am waiting for it to flower, to expose and reveal all its intricacies. For that I must have a little patience, a sense of waiting, watching, being aware, so that the question begins to unfold. As it unfolds, I begin to see the answer. Not that I want an answer, but the question itself starts to unravel and shows me the extraordinary complexity that lies between two human beings who are attracted and perhaps like each other. When we are young, we get sexually involved, and as we grow a little older, we get bored with each other, and gradually escape from that boredom through another person, through divorce – you know all the rest of it. But we find the same problem with another.

You have to have patience. Patience – I mean by that word not allowing time to operate. I don't know if you have gone into the question of patience and impatience. Most of us are rather impatient, and this impatience doesn't give you a deep understanding of problems. Whereas if I have patience, no concern with time, not bothering about ending the problem, I am watching, looking at it, letting it evolve, grow. And with that patience, I begin to find the depth of the answer. Let us do that together now. We are patient, not wanting an immediate answer and our brains are therefore open to looking at and being aware of the problem and its complexity.

What is the root of it? Is it education? Is it that being a man I want to dominate, possess the other? Is it that I am attached so deeply I don't want to let go? And do I see that being tied, attached, will invariably bring about corruption? Corruption in the sense of jealousy, anxiety, fear, wanting – all the consequences of attachment one knows very well. Is that the cause of it, or is it much deeper? First, we mentioned the superficial, then the emotional attachments, and the sentimental, romantic dependency. If I discard all that, is there a still deeper issue involved? We are moving below the superficial and ever deeper so that we can find out for ourselves what the root is. I hope you are doing this with me.

Now, how do I, you, find the root of it? Do you want an answer, want to find the root of it, and therefore making a tremendous effort? Or is your brain quiet, looking? Not agitated, not prey to desire or will, but just watching. Are we doing this together? Just watching to see what the deep cause, the basis is of this conflict between human beings.

Is it the sense of individual separation? Go into this very carefully. Is it the individual concept that I am basically separate from the other? Though biologically we are different, there is also a sense of deep-rooted individual, separative action. Is that the root of it, or is there a still deeper root, a deeper layer? First the sensory, sensual responses, then emotional, romantic and sentimental responses, then attachment with all its corruption. And the profoundly conditioned brain says, 'I am an individual and she is an individual, and being separate entities, each must fulfil in their own way. And the separation is therefore basic.'

Now, is that so? Is it basic? Or have I been educated to *believe* that, to believe that I am an individual and that she, also being an individual, must fulfil herself in her own way, as I do in mine? So, we have already started from the very outset with these two separate directions – they may be running in parallel but never meeting, like two railway lines – and so all I do is try to live harmoniously, struggling with this and never meeting.

If that is the root of it, is separative existence as an individual a reality or is it an illusion I have been nourishing, cherishing, holding onto, without any validity for it? If it lacks validity, I must be absolutely, irrevocably sure that it is an illusion, and ask if the brain can break out of that and realise that psychologically we are all similar. Do you follow? My consciousness is the consciousness of the rest of humanity. Though we differ biologically, consciousness is psychologically similar in all human beings. If I once realise this, not intellectually, but feel it in the depth of my heart, in my blood, in my guts, then my relationship to another undergoes a radical change, inevitably.

We have conflict – must therefore the relationship end?

If we battle with each other all day long, in struggle, in conflict, you know, in bitterness, anger, hatred, repulsion – we bear it as long as we can, and then the moment comes when we have to split. This is a familiar pattern.

What should I do?

If I am everlastingly in conflict with my wife, and somehow cannot patch it up, must the relationship end? Or do I understand basically that the cause of this conflict and disruption is the sense of separate individuality? And having seen the illusory nature of that, I am no longer pursuing the individual line. What takes place when I have perceived that and actually live it? What is my relationship then with the partner who still thinks in terms of the individual?

I see, or she sees – better give this role to her – she sees the foolishness, absurdity, the illusory nature of the individual. She understands it, feels it, and I don't. What takes place between us? She has understood that illusion and I have not. She won't quarrel with me, ever. She won't enter that area at all, but I am constantly pushing her, driving her and trying to pull her into that area. I am creating the conflict, not her. Have you understood how the whole thing has moved? There are now not two people quarrelling but only one. See what has taken place. And if I am at all sensitive, if I have real feeling for her, I also start to change because she is irrevocably there. She will not move out of that.

See what happens. If two immovable objects meet, there is conflict. But if she is immovable and I am movable, I naturally yield to that which is immovable. So, if one has a real understanding of relationship without the image, the problem is resolved. Then by her very presence, her very vitality, her actuality, she is going to transform me.

CHAPTER 10

WOULD YOU PLEASE GO INTO WHAT YOU MEAN BY READING THE BOOK OF YOUR LIFE AT A GLANCE OR WITH A SINGLE LOOK?

I think it is fairly obvious that we human beings are the history of humanity. In us is the totality of all human psychological knowledge.

The story of mankind is wars, tears, bloodshed, pain, grief, laughter, agony, anxiety, pleasure, loneliness, sorrow. All that is part of me: I am that, the story of all that. The book of history is *me*. Not the kings and queens, though they are also part of it. I am all that. Now, do I have to read that book, which is me, page by page, chapter by chapter, not missing a single line until I get to the end?

I am the story of all mankind, that is fairly simple. Do I see that, if only intellectually? The whole of humanity suffers, has wept, has laughed, imitated, conformed, undergone every indignity, vulgarity, superficiality – and I am all that – otherwise I wouldn't elect the politicians we have. I am all that, including the priest, and the gods that thought has invented. I am all that; that book is me. Have I to read it page by page, or can I understand that whole book at one glance, with one single look?

We are saying it is impossible to read that book page by page, chapter by chapter – that will take your whole life, and your life is a period of time. During that time, you are adding more and more; discarding little by little but gathering more and more. The book can never be read page by page. If you understand that, which is logical and objective, if you realise that it cannot be read page by page, then you have only one issue: to look at it with eyes that comprehend from the start to the end at a glance. What does that imply? What does it imply to look at yourself, which is the story of mankind? What does it imply to look at it? Again, this requires patience, to look at it with a patient, silent brain so that the book itself unfolds rapidly.

When you have a map of Switzerland with all the lakes and mountains, and all the beauty of the land, if you have a particular itinerary from Gstaad to Bern, you are only concerned with that route – you don't look at the rest of the map. That is, you go in a particular direction and don't bother to look at the rest of the map. But if you have no direction, you look at all of it. The moment you have a motive that lays down a direction, you look only in that particular direction, but if you have no motive, and so no direction, you look at the whole map at a glance. Now, can you do the same with yourself – anger, jealousy, aggression, attachment, all that? That is the whole map of yourself, which requires quietness of the brain and no direction. Then you see the whole of it clearly. You hear the whole tone of that history and you have captured it immediately, the wholeness of it.

CHAPTER 11

YOU SAID IT IS NECESSARY TO HAVE NO OPINIONS ABOUT ANYTHING, BUT I FEEL IT IS NECESSARY. MUSTN'T ONE SAY SOMETHING ABOUT WHAT IS TAKING PLACE, OR PERHAPS DO SOMETHING?

Why do we have opinions? I am not saying they are necessary or unnecessary, but why do we have them? An opinion is something that has not been proved. Prejudice is a form of opinion. Why do we have them? Not that there is not the spreading of Nazism, of armaments and the use of torture by governments. That is going on; every government is indulging in this in the name of peace, in the name of law, in the name of patriotism, in the name of God. Religions have tortured people. These are facts. Countries are selling armaments to enemies. See the ridiculousness of these facts. And you may have strong opinions against this. So, what are you going to do? Join a group, demonstrate, shout, be beaten up by the police, get pelted with tear gas? You have seen all this happening on television, or have been part of it.

What change have your opinions brought about? The armaments drive has been going on for centuries. They all say we must stop it and yet big business and heavy industry say we can't exist if we don't sell armaments. Will you stop paying taxes? If you do, you are sent to prison. First of all, see the logic of all this. What will you do about these things? They are wrong, cruel and bring about a great deal of violence. No government is free of torturing; they do it more subtly, less obviously, but it goes on. So, what is one to do?

Now, what is an opinion? You have an opinion against all this but what value has that opinion? Will it affect the sale of armaments? Will it prevent Nazism? Will it prevent torture? Or is the whole thing much deeper than merely having opinions? I am not laying down the law or offering an opinion about this because the problem is much deeper than opinions.

A more serious, deeper question is: Why is man against man? Ask that question, not whether opinion is justified or not. Why, after all these centuries of civilization and so-called culture, is man against man? If we could go into that, which requires much more serious inquiry than having opinions or not, we would enter an area where we might do something.

Why are you, as a human being, against another? Why are you against another ideology? You have your own ideology and you are against another. The democratic ideology is at war with the totalitarian ideology. Why do we live by ideologies? Ideologies are not real. They are something invented by thought when you come to a certain philosophical conclusion. After historical, materialistic study, the philosophy becomes law for you and you want others to accept it. And the opposite side does exactly the same thing in a different way. The democratic, so-called free world doesn't put us in prison because we sit and talk like this, while in a totalitarian state we probably wouldn't be able to.

We are asking a fundamental question: Why is man against man? Aren't you against somebody? Aren't you violent? And you are the whole of humanity. I know we like to think we are separate individuals, separate private souls – which we have gone into previously, I won't repeat it – but you are not. You are the rest of mankind because you suffer, agonise, are lonely or depressed like everyone else. You are basically, fundamentally as the rest of mankind. You are humanity, whether you like it or not. You are antagonistic, violent, aggressive, patriotic – my country is better than yours, my culture is the highest, and all that nonsense.

You are a Catholic, you are a Protestant, you are a Hindu, and where there is division there must be conflict.

Are you acting wholly, or as a small, little 'me'? If so, you are man against man.

CHAPTER 12

AFTER LISTENING TO YOU AND THINKING ABOUT
THESE MATTERS ON MY OWN, HOW AM I TO REALLY
NOT JUST SOLVE MY PROBLEMS BUT RADICALLY
BRING ABOUT A CHANGE IN MY LIFE?

The question, to put it very simply, is: What am I to do or not do to bring about a radical mutation in my whole existence? How do you approach that question? How do you draw close to it so that you are in contact with it?

First of all, are you aware that you are conditioned? After two thousand years of steady propaganda – baptism, Mass, constant repetition, repetition, repetition, you have become a Catholic; or through other repetition you are a Hindu or Muslim – it is the same process. Are you aware that your brain is conditioned? It is not difficult to be aware that you are conditioned. When you say, 'I am British' – or German, Russian, French – you are conditioned. The Indian may think, 'I have the greatest culture,' but that culture has gone. In India they are completely at a loss, in disorder – I won't go into that.

So, if you are aware of being conditioned, is that awareness an idea or an actuality? Are you actually aware of your reactions? Don't be puzzled; there is nothing to be puzzled about. Are you aware when you meet somebody that you dislike or like them? Are you aware of your prejudices? Are you aware of your laziness? Are you aware of your incapacity to think clearly? Are you aware of your pretension that you are something extraordinary? Are you aware of all this? If you are, and if you say, 'I like this kind of thing,' then live it; nobody is going to pay much attention to it, at least not intelligent people. You may collect a lot of neurotic, thoughtless people around you – that is also all right if you want that kind of stuff. But the moment you become aware and are watching all your reactions, any correction of those reactions implies an entity who is also a reaction. You have said something and I react to that by hitting you. And then you react because you don't like to be hit. And so on.

When you are aware that you are conditioned, and look at it as an outsider looking in, the very entity that is observing or being aware is part of that conditioning. Like the experiencer and the experience, the observer is not different from the observed. The thinker is not different from thought. The analyser is not different from the thing analysed. Only he has separated himself, so that 'I' examine 'myself'. 'I' is separated by thought as being a little more know-ledgeable, a little more accumulative, and with past memories that entity observes. That entity is part of that which is observed.

Apparently, nothing external or internal changes man. Religions have tried to control him, have tortured him, forced him, put him through baptism and all that circus – and they do this too in their own way in India and other parts of the world. They have tried everything. And you have also tried to bring about a change, haven't you? If you have, and the result is negative, then what do you do? We have tried leaders, gurus, various philosophers and religions, and yet remain as we are: lazy, indolent, indifferent, callous, violent, without a spark of love. What will make us change? *Nothing*. Nothing from outside, nor your own desire to change. Start with the fact that nothing, no agency, inward or outside, is going to change you. Start with that fact. Then you start with something actual, something real, something that you can put your teeth into: nobody is going to help you. The Buddha hasn't helped you. None of the Christian forms of religion have helped you. You are what you are now. Start from there.

Nothing from outside, or your own desire, is going to change you. Start there. Then ask yourself, do I really want to change, basically? Most of us don't, so we just carry on. But if you really want to change, it is simple: end your fears completely. Don't ask how — we went through all that. If you deny totally any help from any form of outside agency, or your own volition, desire or will, and put all that aside, then you start from what you are, and see if that can be changed radically. It is up to you.

CHAPTER 13

HOW DO YOU KNOW WHAT YOU ARE SAYING IS TRUE?

Why do you ask me that? Isn't it true that as long as there is national division, economic division, racial and religious division, there must be conflict? That is a fact. It is not whether what I am saying is true, but facts themselves show what the truth is. As we said previously about relationship, as long as there is separation, psychologically, between two human beings, there must be conflict. That is a fact. So again, it is not how I know what I am saying is true, but it is a fact that as long as I am ambitious, pursuing my particular form of pleasure or fulfilment, and my wife, husband or partner is doing the same thing, we inevitably end up in conflict. That is a fact. So, it isn't how do I know what truth is, but first of all, let us look at facts.

We are people with a great many prejudices, which we cultivate and strengthen vociferously. These prevent us from understanding others. That is a fact. So, can you be free of prejudice, free of the opinions waxing so strongly in our lives? That we can discuss. We can have a conversation, a dialogue, and say, 'I have prejudices, and these prejudices, whatever they are, divide people.' This is a simple fact. And where there is division there must be conflict. Those who are bigoted must be in conflict – it is a fact. I have nothing to do with it, so it isn't how do I know what I am saying is true – we are just facing facts.

Now, what is a fact? What do you think a fact is? That which has happened, an incident, a car accident, that is a fact. And what is happening now is a fact. But what will happen in the future may not be a fact. So, a fact implies that which has already happened.

Yesterday, walking along the lane, I met a viper. It didn't bite me. That is a fact. And what is happening now, what I am thinking and doing now, is a fact. And what I will do in future may not be a fact: it might or might not happen.

If we are now clear what a fact is, then what is an idea? Is an idea a fact? We usually see a fact then make an abstraction, an idea of it, and then pursue the idea. This means there is a conclusion from the fact and then we stick to that conclusion, not staying with the understanding of the fact.

So please, it is not how do you know what you are saying is true – I am merely pointing out facts. Those facts are not personal. If I say I am a Hindu and I stick to it, that is a fact. It is an illusion, a kind of superstitious, sentimental nonsense, but it is also fact. A fact can be an illusion or actual. Most of us live with illusions. I am an Indian – that is an illusion – and you, if I may most gently point out, are British – which is also an illusion. And this tribal, insular worship is destroying the world. That is a fact. As long as I am an Arab and you are something else, I am going to destroy you, because I believe that by destroying you I will go to heaven. That is an illusion accepted as a fact, and for that illusion, people are willing to fight, kill and destroy.

So, can we always deal with facts? I will repeat that: Can we always be with facts, not translate the facts according to my prejudice, my beliefs, my neurotic illusions, however noble they are? Can I look at the facts and understand what those facts are saying?

Suppose I had an accident in my car. Can I look at the fact that I was rather careless, driving too fast, not paying full attention because I was talking to my friend next to me, instead of saying, 'It wasn't my fault, that other driver is a fool'?

Now, it is a fact that we have ideals. Don't you have ideals? I am afraid you do. What are those ideals? Are

131

they facts? The ideal that we must live peacefully, that we must – whatever it is – be non-violent, or the ideals of a communist derived from a historical study prejudiced by conditioning. Why do we have ideals at all? I know this is a dangerous thing to say because most of us live with these extraordinary ideals.

We are questioning. Please, I am not saying you should or shouldn't have them. I am saying, *why* do we have them? Ideals, faiths, beliefs, as a Christian, Buddhist, Hindu, American, Indian, and all the rest of it – why? Is it that our brain is incapable of living without illusion? What do you say to that? Is your brain strong, vital, capable of understanding things as they are without creating a future ideal? An ideal is non-existent. Christians and all religious people believe that you must not kill, and Christians have probably killed more than anybody else. And so it goes on, even though we know that ideals, faiths and beliefs of every kind divide people. That is a fact.

Can we be free of ideals, of faith, of being identified with one group versus another group, which other people have identified with? Can we be free of all this? Can we, or is it impossible? Is it possible or impossible? Why it is impossible? Is it possible to have a free brain that is not cluttered with a lot of rubbish, a lot of illusions? Some may say no, it is impossible because I cannot live without my beliefs. I must have my ideals, my faith, otherwise I am lost. Yet in your faith, ideals and beliefs you are already lost. That is a fact. We are lost people. Why do I cling to my particular prejudice, particular ideal, and so on? Why have I identified myself with them? Why do I identify myself with anything? Push deeply into it to find out why we do all these things. Why have we allowed ourselves to be programmed? Why we are afraid of public opinion?

So, the question of how do you know what you are saying is true has, I am afraid, very little meaning. Truth is not something mysterious, truth is where you are. From there we can begin. The truth is I am angry, jealous, aggressive, quarrelsome. That is a fact. You must start, if I may most respectfully point out, from where you are. That is why it is important to know, to have complete knowledge of yourself, not from others, not from psychologists, the brain experts and so on, but knowing what you are. Because you are the story of mankind. If you know how to read that book, which is yourself, then you know all the activities, brutalities and stupidities of humanity, because you are the rest of the world.

Sources

Part 1

1. Saanen 1983, Talk 1
2. Saanen 1983, Talk 2
3. Saanen 1983, Talk 3
4. Saanen 1983, Talk 4
5. Saanen 1983, Talk 5
6. Saanen 1983, Talk 6

Part 2

Introduction: Saanen 1983, Q&A 3

7. Saanen 1981, Q&A 1
8. Saanen 1981, Q&A 1
9. Saanen 1981, Q&A 3
10. Saanen 1981, Q&A 3
11. Saanen 1983, Q&A 3
12. Saanen 1983, Q&A 3
13. Brockwood 1983, Q&A 1

About the Author

Krishnamurti spoke not as a guru but as a friend, and his talks and discussions are based not on tradition-based knowledge but on his own insights into the human mind and his vision of the sacred. He left a large body of literature in the form of public talks, writings, discussions with teachers and students, scientists and religious figures, conversations with individuals, television and radio interviews, and letters. Many of these have been published as books, and audio and video recordings.

For more information, please visit kfoundation.org.